A
heart
on
fire

"I invite everyone to renew his devotion to the Sacred Heart of Christ in the month of June, making use of the traditional prayer of the offering of the day and keeping in mind the intentions that I have proposed to the whole Church."

Pope Benedict XVI
Angelus Address, June 1, 2008

"Father Kubicki helps readers place their hearts into the glorious Heart of Jesus through Eucharistic worship and its extension, devotion to the Sacred Heart."

Cardinal Raymond L. Burke
Prefect of the Apostolic Signatura

"At first communion I was taught to say first thing every morning, 'Sacred Heart of Jesus, I place all my trust in Thee!' Reading Father Kubicki's splendid book has only made that prayer all the more sincere and meaningful."

Cardinal Timothy M. Dolan
Archbishop of New York

"Fr. James Kubicki's book on devotion to the Sacred Heart of Jesus presents a fresh and attractive reconsideration of this centuries-old devotion in the Catholic Church. Blessed Basile Moreau († 1873), founder of the Congregation of Holy Cross, who entrusted his priests to the Sacred Heart of Jesus, wrote: 'The primary purpose of the devotion to the Sacred Heart is to return love for love.' Fr. Kubicki develops this theme in a way that speaks well to today's generation of believers."

Rev. Peter D. Rocca, C.S.C.
Rector, Basilica of the Sacred Heart
University of Notre Dame

"This accessible presentation of the Sacred Heart devotion grounds it in God's devotion to us and links it to the Eucharist. The many practical devotions and prayers help us see our everyday lives as a prayer offered to God."

Celia Wolf-Devine
Author of *The Heart Transformed*

"At a time when many people are losing heart, Fr. Kubicki's book, *A Heart on Fire*, reminds us to be rooted and grounded in the 'True Love Story,' the Heart of Jesus. This book will revive many hearts!"

Kathleen Beckman
Magnificat, A Ministry to Catholic Women

"The beautiful and succinct combination of Scriptural understanding, historical background, spiritual reflections, and prayer exercises in this book leads us to a new appreciation and deep love for the Sacred Heart of Jesus."

Vicki Thorn
Founder
Project Rachel

Rediscovering Devotion
to the
SACRED
HEART of JESUS

A
heart
on
fire

JAMES KUBICKI, S.J.

ave maria press AMP notre dame, indiana

Imprimi Potest
Very Rev. Thomas A. Lawler, Provincial
Wisconsin Province of the Society of Jesus

Founded in 1865, Ave Maria Press is a ministry of the United States Province of Holy Cross.

www.avemariapress.com

Paperback: ISBN-10 1-59471-287-5   ISBN-13 978-1-59471-287-6

E-book: ISBN-10 1-59471-345-6   ISBN-13 978-1-59471-345-3

Cover and text design by John R. Carson.

Printed and bound in the United States of America.

Library of Congress Cataloging-in-Publication Data

Kubicki, James.
  A heart on fire : rediscovering devotion to the sacred heart of Jesus / James Kubicki.
    p. cm.
  Includes bibliographical references (p.   ).
  ISBN 978-1-59471-287-6 (pbk.) -- ISBN 1-59471-287-5 (pbk.)
  1. Sacred Heart, Devotion to. I. Title.
  BX2157.K83 2012
  232--dc23
                    2012001147

Contents

1 / The Heart

Many people think the Sacred Heart of Jesus is an old-fashioned Catholic devotion that doesn't speak to anyone anymore. Some dismiss the devotion because of the way the Heart of Jesus is portrayed in art. A pierced and bleeding heart, for example, surrounded with thorns and presented apart from any physical body just doesn't appeal to some people. Other depictions of the Sacred Heart, trying to emphasize the tender love of Jesus with a wispy beard and doe-like eyes, make him look effeminate. In some popular images of fifty or a hundred years ago, you see flowers and cups and angels. Some artists, reacting against such sentimental portraits of Jesus, created images that are almost abstract, sometimes rendering the image obscure or devoid of meaning.

Increasingly, you can see Sacred Heart images that present Jesus in the style of an Eastern Orthodox icon, inviting the viewer to pray. Unfortunately, in these icons Jesus often appears stern and severe, like the all-powerful judge in the well-known icon Christ Pantocrator.

Stern images of Jesus take us in the opposite direction from the warm and inviting Jesus who said, "Come to me, all you who labor and are burdened, and I will give you rest. Take my yoke upon you and learn from me, for I am meek and humble of heart" (Mt 11:28–29).

Art is a matter of personal taste, and our tastes change, both personally and in the wider culture. This is especially true of our tastes in religious art. As an adult, we may no longer like the image of the Sacred Heart that we liked as a child. Encountering an image we have never seen before, we may not like the face, the hair, the clothing, the background, or the way an image invites us to think of Jesus.

We have a right to dislike any images of the Sacred Heart we please. But let's not throw the baby out with the bath water. Images of the Sacred Heart of Jesus are not the actual Heart of Christ—the divine and human heart that loves us as no one else can. As we get to know Jesus, we will find that to the eyes of our spirit his heart is unspeakably beautiful. Whatever our taste in images, we do not have to miss the deeper reality of the Sacred Heart. In this book, I focus on the meaning of the Heart of Jesus. My hope is that you will grow in devotion to the Heart of Christ, a devotion that is based on understanding. With a deeper understanding of the meaning of the Sacred Heart of Jesus, I am confident that sooner or later you will also discover images of the Sacred Heart that you find beautiful.

A Universal Symbol

The heart is a universal symbol. Right after the Christmas decorations leave the stores, we see red and pink hearts all over the place. The preparations for Valentine's Day begin with cards filled with hearts and candy shaped liked hearts. No one asks, "Why? Why all the hearts?" On a day that's designated for declaring one's affection, romantic attraction, or love, giving a card or box of candy shaped like a heart says something we all understand.

And then there are the buttons, T-shirts, bumper stickers, and posters with "I ♥ my schnauzer" or "I ♥ the Big Apple." We say we ♥ whatever it is we really like, whatever makes us feel good.

Popular music is filled with references to the heart. Bruce Springsteen declared, "Everybody's got a hungry heart," while Janis Joplin (and Faith Hill) sang, "Take another little piece of my heart." Obviously they weren't singing about the blood-pumping muscle in their bodies. When we hear these words, we know they're talking about something more than a physical organ. U2 sang "Two hearts beat as one," and we all understand this as the expression of the deep mutual love of lovers. The Backstreet Boys sang that "even in my heart, I see you're not bein' true to me. . . . Quit playin' games with my heart."

Be faithful in small things because it is in them that your strength lies. Nothing is small for our good God, for he is great and we are small.

Blessed Teresa of Calcutta

The lover's heartfelt complaint is about someone playing games with his affections. It's also significant that in his heart he "sees" or recognizes her unfaithfulness, for the heart is a most reliable way to know the truth.

Our language is filled with such expressions. Someone who has no compassion for others is said to be "cold-hearted" or "heartless" and is challenged by one in need to "have a heart." Compassionate people are said to be "all heart" and if they are moved to the point of tears, they may be said to "wear their hearts on their sleeves." A person with a "big heart" does not need surgery on an enlarged heart. It's just a way that we say that someone has a lot of love for others. When we feel sorry for another we say, "My heart goes out to you." It's a way of saying that my deepest center, the place from which I love, sees and shares your pain.

The feelings of one's heart, though sometimes sentimental, run deeper than the strongest emotions. The heart is not passive. The heart makes decisions. From the heart, acts of the will arise. So it's no surprise that the virtue we call courage is found in the heart. In fact, the word *courage* is derived from the Latin word for heart, *cor*. And so we exhort someone who is struggling to persevere in the face of difficulties, "Take heart!"

When people experience a conversion or make a major change in something they have previously decided, we say that they have had "a change of heart." The phrase "change of heart" doesn't mean they have had a heart transplant, but they have simply undergone a change in their inner self that has led to a change in their choices and behavior.

A person who is good and faithful is said to have a "heart of gold." The symbol of the heart has lost none of its meaning and power despite the rush of modern times. The heart is a universal and perennial symbol. More than conveying a romantic feeling, it symbolizes courage and compassion. The heart is the symbol of true love, that love for which every human being is searching. Yet, we so often look for love in the wrong places. And our use of the heart symbol on our T-shirts and bumper stickers shows that we have a confused idea of love. We "love" whatever gives us pleasure. But is this true love? The fact that we keep searching indicates that it isn't.

Hungry Hearts

Bruce Springsteen's song "Hungry Heart" with its line, "Everybody's got a hungry heart," has to do with a man restlessly looking for romantic love, but it points to something more. Romantic love may fill one's heart for a while and take away the hunger, but it is not enough. Nothing earthly satisfies. Made in the image and likeness of God who is Love itself, we are built for infinite love—a love that begins here on earth and finds fulfillment hereafter. Our loving union with God, which expands into a love for our neighbor, starts now. Our hearts are being transformed as we learn what Jesus taught. "You shall love the Lord, your God, with all your heart, with all your soul, and with all your mind. This is the greatest and the first commandment. The second is like it: You shall love your neighbor as yourself" (Mt 22:37–39).

In his autobiography, *The Confessions*, St. Augustine wrote famously that "you have made us for yourself, O Lord, and our hearts are restless until they rest in you." We will always have a hungry heart this side of eternity. Even though we do experience the joy of union with God and love of neighbor, there will always be a hole in our hearts that only God can fill. We may turn to all kinds of substitutes, but they ultimately don't satisfy.

In the First Letter of John, we read that "God is Love" (1 Jn 4:8). In God's image and likeness, we're made *by* love and we're made *for* love. We're made to know God's love and to love in return. And if we truly love God, then we will love what God loves—our neighbors. The greatest commandment is one commandment—love, a love that is not sentimental or selfish—a love that is divine. Such love is possible only insofar as it originates in the heart of God who is Love.

> *We must enlarge our hearts in imitation of the Heart of Jesus. How much hard work this is! However, it is the only thing needed, and when this is done, everything is done. It is a matter of loving each person we meet as God loves him or her.*
>
> **Chiara Lubich**

God's Kind of Love

I believe that most people don't understand God's kind of love. For many, many people, the heart symbol declares that "whatever makes me feel good—my dog or my car or my kayak—I love! Whatever or whoever gives me pleasure, I love!" The real meaning is that it's all about ME. There's nothing wrong with enjoying and having strong affection for our dog or our sports team or the zoo, but it's sad when we define our love of something or someone only by the pleasure we receive. We are in danger of falling in love only for ourselves, excluding God and others.

In his first encyclical, *God Is Love* (*Deus Caritas Est*), Pope Benedict recognized that there is a problem with our understanding of the word *love*. He wrote, "Today, the term *love* has become one of the most frequently used and misused of words, a word to which we attach quite different meanings" (*DCE*, 2). And then the pope went on to give us a definition for true love, pointing to the pierced side of Christ (Jn 19:37). "It is from there that our definition of love must begin" (*DCE*, 12). If we go to the pierced side of Jesus, we will find the way to true love. We will enter the Sacred Heart of Jesus.

Devotion to Christ's Heart is neither outdated nor unnecessary. God's Heart is at the core, the heart of our Christian life. Devotion to the Sacred Heart of Jesus is grounded in scripture and tradition. It is eucharistic and transforming.

Pope Pius XI's 1928 encyclical, *On Reparation to the Sacred Heart* (*Miserentissimus Redemptor*), says this about the devotion to the Sacred Heart of Jesus:

> Is not a summary of all our religion and, moreover, a guide to a more perfect life contained in this one devotion? Indeed, it more easily leads our minds to know Christ the Lord intimately and more effectively turns our hearts to love Him more ardently and to imitate Him more perfectly. (*MR*, 3)

A Prayer for You

As you read this book, my prayer for you is St. Paul's prayer for the Ephesians. The Letter to the Ephesians (like those to the Colossians, Philippians, and Philemon) is called a "captivity" epistle, for it was written while Paul was in prison in Rome. Paul knew the Church of Ephesus well, having spent two years there. It's likely that news of his imprisonment caused the community members consternation. Would they too be thrown into prison? This is the context for Paul's prayer. He makes it clear in the verse that precedes the prayer. "I ask you not to lose heart over my afflictions for you; this is your glory" (Eph 3:13). Then Paul writes this beautiful prayer.

For this reason I kneel before the Father, from whom every family in heaven and on earth is named, that he may grant you in accord with the riches of his glory to be strengthened with power through his Spirit in the inner self, and that Christ may dwell in your hearts through faith; that you, rooted and grounded in love, may have strength to comprehend with all the holy ones what is the breadth and length and height and depth, and to know the love of Christ that surpasses knowledge, so that you may be filled with all the fullness of God. Now to him who is able to accomplish far more than all we ask or imagine, by the power at work within us, to him be glory in the church and in Christ Jesus to all generations, forever and ever. Amen. (Eph 3:14–21)

Paul is afraid that the Ephesians will "lose heart," lose their courage and hope, and fall away from the faith. So he kneels before the Father of Jesus, source of all life and holiness. He prays that their "inner self" may be strengthened by the Holy Spirit, which is the very bond of love between the Father and the Son.

In Paul's prayer, the inner self is the heart. According to Pope Benedict XVI, "in biblical language, heart indicates the center of the person where his sentiments and intentions dwell" (Angelus Address, June 5, 2005). At another occasion, he said that "in accordance with the Bible and the Fathers [of the Church], the heart is the intimate depths of man, the place in which God dwells" (General Audience, June 13, 2007). In the Hebrew scriptures, the word *heart* (*lēb*) is the most common term used for the deepest reality of a person. The word for heart occurs 814 times, more than the Hebrew word for *soul* (*nepeš*), which occurs 755 times.

> *For a Christian the heart represents the fountain of all his personal life, where thought, love, and sentiments converge into one:* Cor meum, *says St. Augustine,* ubi sum, quicumque sum: *"My heart, where I am, whatever I am."*
>
> **Pedro Arrupe, S.J.**

After praying that the hearts of the Ephesians be filled with the power of the Holy Spirit, Paul prays "that Christ may dwell in your hearts through faith" (Eph 3:17). He asks that their hearts may become homes for Jesus. And I pray the same for you. Through the angel Gabriel, Mary received the Word of God into her heart and then conceived the Word in her womb. We too are to have hearts open to the Word of God. This is faith—a loving surrender to God's Word, God's will in our lives. When we receive the Word into our hearts, we give flesh to him in our lives.

In this way we are "rooted and grounded in love." With Paul, I pray that God's love will become the foundation of your life, the basis for all your choices. I pray that you will not be controlled by fear or self-preoccupation, but be empowered by the love of God revealed in Jesus. Rooted in this way, you will bear good fruit for, as Jesus told his disciples at the Last Supper, "I am the vine, you are the branches. Whoever remains in me and I in him will bear much fruit, because without me you can do nothing" (Jn 15:5).

The Heart's Wisdom

One of the fruits of being rooted and grounded in love is wisdom. Wisdom is not so much knowledge of the head as of the heart. God and "the love of Christ" surpass all knowledge. With human reason, symbolized by the head, we can learn about people and things, but by reason alone we can never really know them. We can know things *about* a person without truly knowing that person. Deeper knowledge of someone is attained only through the heart. As Pope Benedict once said when he was still known as Joseph Cardinal Ratzinger, "You only see properly with your heart." He was quoting from a classic children's book, *The Little Prince*, which warns that in our adult head,

> *It is only with the heart that one can see rightly; what is essential is invisible to the eye.*
>
> **Antoine de Saint-Exupéry**

knowledge can easily get in the way of the childlike wisdom of our hearts. Jesus prayed, "I give praise to you, Father, Lord of heaven and earth, for although you have hidden these things from the wise and the learned you have revealed them to the childlike" (Mt 11:25). Later, as his disciples vied for positions of worldly power and glory, he placed a child in their midst and said, "Amen, I say to you, unless you turn and become like children, you will not enter the kingdom of heaven" (Mt 18:3).

Revealing Love

If we are to truly know someone, that person needs to reveal him- or herself to us. And then we must be humbly receptive to what that person says to us in words and deeds. As this is true in human relations, it is also true in our relationship with God. We come to know God deeply by our hearts, not our heads. Knowledge of God is true wisdom because it knows, not simply outward appearance and personal data, but also the interior of another. It's like the difference between an optometrist looking into the eyes of a patient and a lover looking into the eyes of the beloved. Both have knowledge of the other, but the lover has the truer, deeper knowledge of the heart.

To know God and not just about God we need God to reveal himself to us. God does this through Jesus, "the human face" of God as Pope Benedict likes to say, and through the Holy Spirit. For, as Paul wrote, "Among human beings, who knows what pertains to a person except the spirit of the person that is within? Similarly, no one knows what pertains to God except the Spirit of God" (1 Cor 2:11). We need the Holy Spirit to guide and strengthen us, to overshadow us, so that Christ may dwell in us and fill us with intimate knowledge of himself and his love, which surpasses all our human capacities to understand.

In coming to know Christ, we come to know not only God but also ourselves, since Jesus is truly and fully God and truly and fully human. As the Second Vatican Council states in its pastoral constitution *The Church in the Modern World* (*Gaudium et Spes*), "The truth is that only in the mystery of the incarnate Word does the mystery of man take on light. . . . Christ . . . by the revelation of the mystery of the Father and His love, fully reveals man to man himself and makes his supreme calling clear" (*GS*, 22). To know oneself and one's end or goal in life is true wisdom—knowledge of the heart more than the head. This is why in the Hebrew scriptures the word for heart appears more often in the Wisdom books such as Proverbs and Ecclesiastes than in the books of the law or the prophets.

Having this wisdom, this knowledge of ourselves and of God, we "earthen vessels" will attain something that we could never have imagined (2 Cor 4:7). We will "be filled with the fullness of God." Like Mary, we will be "full of grace" and God's presence. It begins in Baptism where we are transformed into the beloved children of the Father, not just in name but also in reality. John, Jesus' beloved disciple, declares, "See what love the Father has bestowed on us that we may be called the children of God. Yet so we are" (1 Jn 3:1). Or, as Paul wrote, "Do you not know that you are a temple of God, and that the Spirit of God dwells in you?" (1 Cor 3:16). Where One Person of the Trinity dwells, the Three Persons dwell. This indwelling of God is nurtured through the Holy Eucharist where Jesus comes to us and joins his flesh to ours, making us one.

All this knowledge of love is beyond our comprehension. So we must become humble, like children totally dependent upon their loving parents, in order to receive the revelation of the Word-Made-Flesh within us. How God transforms us with love is beyond our imagining. Contrasting human and divine wisdom, St. Paul quotes Isaiah, "But as it is written: 'What eye has not seen, and ear has not heard, and what has not entered the human heart, what God has prepared for those who love him,' this God has revealed to us through the Spirit" (1 Cor 2:9–10; Is 64:3).

God's infinite love is beyond what our minds can conceive, but with our hearts open to the Holy Spirit's "power at work within us," love accomplishes all we need. So like St. Paul in the last verse of his prayer, we do not pat ourselves on the back but give all the glory to God.

Afraid that the Ephesians might "lose heart," St. Paul prays in these eight verses that they may "take heart." He prays for us as well. Likewise, I pray for you.

In the coming chapters, we enter into what I like to call the True Love Story, the account of the Sacred Heart of Jesus as it comes to us in the scriptures and through the Church. We see how we may encounter the Heart of Jesus today in word and sacrament, especially the Holy Eucharist. I propose ways that you can grow in union with the Heart of Jesus and show how this union can change your daily life. We also reflect on the surprising communal dimension of devotion to the Sacred Heart and take a new look at some traditional practices associated with it.

As you enter more deeply into what has come to be known as devotion to the Sacred Heart of Jesus, I pray that you will be more aware of the Heart that the Lord asks you to receive, that Heart which is his and which he desires to unite with your own. In that way, in the words of the U2 song, your "two hearts will beat as one." United to the Heart of Jesus, your heart will be transformed, and you will be "filled with the utter fullness of God."

Prayer Exercise

Praying with an Image of the Sacred Heart of Jesus

As followers of Christ, our desire is to unite our hearts with his. This meditative prayer helps us do that by using the image of the Heart of Jesus as it is traditionally represented on the outside of his body—with thorns, cross, wound, and fire.

1. Look at the Heart of Jesus. Why do you think it appears on the outside of his body? A child once said, "Maybe he loves us so much he can't keep it inside."

   Jesus' heart goes out to you. He does not hide his love. He makes himself vulnerable to you. His love is there for you to touch. The only barriers to his love for you are the ones you put around your own heart. Let down those barriers and meet Jesus heart to heart.

2. Look at the thorns that encircle the Heart of Jesus. This is no sentimental Valentine heart, for instead of lace we see thorns. The thorns signify his passion for you. If you were the only person in the world, he would have suffered and died just for love of you.

   Remember how the soldiers crowned Jesus with thorns and mocked him. The world often despises vulnerable love. Have you been despised or disrespected for loving vulnerably? If so, you are suffering as Jesus did. Jesus shares your suffering.

3. Look at the cross on top of the image of the Heart of Jesus. Most of Jesus' friends ran away and would not stand under his cross, but his mother did, along with St. John, who called himself the "disciple whom Jesus loved." Will you stand with them under that cross?

   It is not easy to watch a person suffer and die. You don't need to say anything. It is enough simply to be with Jesus now. Your being there lets him know of your love. His being there lets you know of his. If he could have shown his love for you in a more convincing way, he would have.

4. Look at the wound on the Heart of Jesus. As Jesus hung on the cross, his side was pierced by a lance that also opened his heart. Blood and water poured from his wound, signifying the new life we have in Baptism and the Eucharist.

   People try to hide their wounds, but the wounds of Jesus remain on his resurrected body, eternal signs of his love. The wound on his heart is a sign of his love for you. Touch this wound with your heart, and, like the Apostle Thomas, believe in the love of the One who suffered, died, and rose again.

5. Look at the fire blazing from the Heart of Jesus. Peer into its light and feel its warmth. The blazing Heart of Jesus reveals to you how precious you are. The fire of his love kindles its warmth deep inside of you.

Resolve that you will no more allow your heart to become stone cold and hard. You will come often to the burning Heart of Jesus. You will catch his fire and return his love with all your heart. His fire will become your fire, and you will go forth setting the world on fire.

2 / **The True Love Story**

Many people think that Sacred Heart devotion began in the seventeenth century with a Visitation nun named St. Margaret Mary Alacoque. The reality is that it began much earlier. In fact, it began before time began, in the eternal Heart of God.

Sacred Heart devotion isn't our devotion. It's God's. It's God's devotion to us. Our devotion is only a response to God's devoted love, because God loved us first. The Apostle John, who often refers to himself as the disciple "whom Jesus loved," wrote, "God is love" (1 Jn 4:8, 16). Behind this phrase is the great mystery of God's identity. God is a communion of three loving divine persons, a Trinity of love. In this communion of love, God needs no one else's love. Yet, the nature of all love is to share, and so God created a world with which he could share his life and love. So devotion to the Sacred Heart of Jesus begins with God, the Creative Lover, who makes a world with creatures who are capable of receiving love. As those creatures understand how God loves them, they naturally return God's love. This is how God always wanted it to be.

> *The living and true God tirelessly calls each person to that mysterious encounter known as prayer. In prayer, the faithful God's initiative of love always comes first; our own first step is always a response.*
>
> **The Catechism of the Catholic Church, 2567**

After stating that "God is love," John continues, "In this is love: not that we have loved God, but that he has loved us. . . . We love because he first loved us" (1 Jn 4:10, 19). Without changing the basic idea, we could rephrase John's words, "In this is our devotion: not that we are devoted to the Sacred Heart of Jesus, but that his heart has been devoted to us. We have devotion because he was first and always devoted to us."

The Measure of God's Love

The depth of our devotion to God is proportional to our understanding and acceptance of God's loving devotion to us. Diadochus, a fifth-century Greek bishop, helped establish the Hesychast or heart-centered spirituality of eastern Christianity. In *On Spiritual Perfection*, important both in the eastern and the western Churches, Diadochus wrote that "anyone who loves God in the depths of his heart has already been loved by God. In fact, the measure of a man's love for God depends upon how deeply aware he is of God's love for him."

So, if that is the measure of someone's love for God, what is the measure of God's love for us? There is no measure. God's love for us is infinite. This is the True Love Story that begins in the Heart of God. It begins when God created human beings in his own image and likeness. Made by love itself and for love, we humans were made for union with God and to be part of a communion of persons that mirrors the love of the Trinity. This was God's original plan. Only one more thing was necessary. Besides God (the lover) and humanity (the beloved), the plan required that humanity, like God, be free.

Without freedom, love is impossible. Even God could not pro-gram human beings to love; robots cannot love. Love requires the free choice to love. And God would not pull the strings when human beings chose to do the opposite of love; puppets are incapable of love. God could not hold a gun to the heads of human beings and demand of them, "Love me!" Our response would not be one of love, but of fear. Love cannot be forced. When God created human beings with free will, he took the risk that in exercising their freedom, they would reject his love. And so it happened. The original plan of love was sabotaged by sin, the first sin, original sin.

The Rebellion

The third chapter of Genesis describes how human beings rejected love, turning away from God. What happened with the first humans shows exactly how sin works for all of us. Doubt and fear led our ancestral parents to reject God's love. Adam and Eve had a loving and trusting relationship with God at the beginning. But something evil engaged the woman in a seemingly innocent conversation about which fruit from the trees in paradise could be eaten. The evil one appealed to her head, sowing doubt in her mind. Seeking to disrupt the love for God in their hearts, the evil one subtly suggested that God may not have told them the whole story, that God may have even lied to them.

The temptation of the evil one involved a lie, a good that was dis-torted, a truth that was twisted. True love requires a certain equality between the two parties. As much as we can say that we love our pets, this affection is not the true love that exists between spouses who share an equal human nature. God created us for love, for true love, but that implies a certain equality. The evil one tempted Eve to think that God did not want such love, that God wanted to keep them ignorant of good and evil so that they would be completely subservient to him. Wouldn't it be better to be like God, knowing good and evil from experience and determining for themselves what is good and what is bad for them? By knowing good and evil, they could be God's equals. Then they would be capable of a truly loving relationship.

We know the rest of the story. Adam and Eve rejected God's plan and grasped at equality with God, something that he planned to give them as a gift through sanctifying grace. It would make them truly his sons and daughters. They did not trust God and did not wait for God's gift. This first rebellion against God's plan and rejection of his love has been replayed throughout history. The original sin involves the separation of head from heart. When we sin we say, in so many words, "I want love, because that's what I'm made for, but I don't want your love or your way of love. I'll find it on my own. I'll do it my way, God."

> *The greatest tragedy of our world is that men do not know, really know, that God loves them.*
>
> **Catherine de Hueck Doherty**

But there is no real substitute for God's love. God's love is true and nourishing food, and until we receive it, we will always have a restless and hungry heart. Substitutes may take away the hunger pains for a time, but ultimately, like junk food, they don't nourish us and, in the long run, they harm us.

God's Response

Rejected by humanity, did God return the favor and reject us? No. God is love and continues to love us passionately. His passion for us ultimately led to his passion and crucifixion, God's ultimate act of love for sinners, his extravagant attempt to save us from ourselves.

John's words, "In this is love: not that we have loved God but that he has loved us," continue, "and sent his Son as expiation for our sins" (1 Jn 4:10). God did not abandon humanity, nor abandon his plan to share his love. God set out to prove his love in as convincing a way as possible. God could not impose his plan on us because to do so would ruin the loving relationship for which God created us. Instead, God "proposed" to us.

Does the idea of God proposing to humanity as a young man proposes to his beloved strike you as odd or even scandalous? Do you find it strange to think of God's love for humanity in terms of passionate desire? It shouldn't. The Hebrew scriptures are filled with marital imagery to express God's love for his Chosen People. The prophet Isaiah, speaking God's word, writes,

> You shall be a glorious crown in the hand of the Lord,
>   a royal diadem held by your God.
> No more shall men call you "Forsaken,"
>   or your land "Desolate,"
> But you shall be called "My Delight,"
>   and your land "Espoused."
> For the Lord delights in you,
>   and makes your land his spouse.
> As a young man marries a virgin,
>   your Builder shall marry you;
> And as a bridegroom rejoices in his bride
>   so shall your God rejoice in you. (Is 62:3–5)

Have you ever imagined God calling you "My Delight"? Because you are unique, there is no other person on the face of the earth (moreover there never has been and never will be) who can give God the "delight" that you give him. God desires an intimate relationship with you.

The Nature of God's Love

Pope Benedict wrote about the love of God in his encyclical *God Is Love (DCE)* and in his Message for Lent in 2007, using two Greek words for love. English has only one word for love. Perhaps that is the reason we are often confused about the nature of love and end up using that word to describe all sorts of feelings and experiences. But in Greek there are several words for love, and two of them—*eros* and *agape*—describe the love that is in God's heart. They capture the essence of God's devotion to humanity, a devotion that is both passionate and self-sacrificing.

From the word *eros* we get the English word *erotic*. So it's more than a little surprising to think that God loves us with an eros love, but in itself eros is not necessarily sinful. God created humans with erotic desires, and it was only after the original sin that these desires became corrupted. Eros in humanity tended to be self-seeking, unlike God's eros love for us, his passionate desire that always seeks our good, our joy. Made in God's likeness, we too are erotic by nature; but, because we tend toward sin, our erotic nature falls far short of God's.

Pope Benedict shows how the Hebrew scriptures, especially the Song of Songs and the Prophets, reveal the eros of God. "The Prophets, particularly Hosea and Ezekiel, described God's passion for his people using boldly erotic images. God's relationship with Israel is described using the metaphors of betrothal and marriage; idolatry is thus adultery and prostitution" (*DCE,* 9). Sin distorts what should be sacred. Our erotic desires for another person lead us into impurity and even adultery. Sin also distorts what should be our sacred erotic desire for God, leading us into idolatry.

In Greek terms, God's love is agape as well as eros. *Agape* means self-sacrificing love. Pope Benedict writes, "We have seen that God's eros for man is also totally agape. This is not only because it is bestowed in a completely gratuitous manner, without any previous merit, but also because it is love which forgives. . . . God's passionate love for his people—for humanity—is at the same time a forgiving love" (*DCE,* 10). God's devotion to his people is so great that he gives his all, his own Son who sacrificed himself on the cross. In the words of a contemporary Christian song by Jody McBrayer, "You would rather die / than to ever live without me."

In his Lenten Message for 2007, Pope Benedict returned to this line of thought.

> The term *agape*, which appears many times in the New Testament, indicates the self-giving love of one who looks exclusively for the good of the other. The word *eros*, on the

other hand, denotes the love of one who desires to possess what he or she lacks and yearns for union with the beloved. The love with which God surrounds us is undoubtedly agape. . . . But God's love is also eros.

Then, referring us to both Hosea and Ezekiel, Benedict writes, "These biblical texts indicate that eros is part of God's very Heart: the Almighty awaits the 'yes' of his creatures as a young bridegroom that of his bride."

Pope Benedict went on to say that the eros and agape of God unite on the cross.

> It is in the mystery of the Cross that the overwhelming power of the Heavenly Father's mercy is revealed in all of its fullness. In order to win back the love of his creature, he accepted to pay a very high price: the Blood of his Only Begotten Son. . . . On the Cross, God's eros for us is made manifest. . . . Dear brothers and sisters, let us look at Christ pierced on the Cross! He is the unsurpassing revelation of God's love, a love in which eros and agape, far from being opposed, enlighten each other. On the Cross, it is God himself who begs the love of his creature: He is thirsty for the love of every one of us. The Apostle Thomas recognized Jesus as "Lord and God" when he put his hand into the wound of his side. Not surprisingly, many of the saints found in the Heart of Jesus the deepest expression of this mystery of love. One could rightly say that the revelation of God's eros toward man is, in reality, the supreme expression of his agape.

Christian faith, in its essence, is a love affair between God and man. Not just a simple love affair: It is a passionate love affair.

Catherine de Hueck Doherty

For Pope Benedict, God's passionate desire for humanity, his devotion revealed on the cross, invites a loving response from us. Love desires to be loved in return. Love goes to the extreme of proving its love, and hopes that this love will be received and returned.

God wants only to love and to know that his love has been received, not rejected. In the words of Pope Benedict, "The response the Lord ardently desires of us is above all that we welcome his love and allow ourselves to be drawn to him."

In both *God Is Love* and his Lenten Message of 2007, Pope Benedict wrote about how the prophet Hosea anticipated the passionate love of God that leads to his Passion and Death on the cross. In a 1981 talk at a Sacred Heart conference in Toulouse, France, Pope Benedict spoke of how the Heart of God is broken at humanity's rejection. Drawing on research of Heinrich Gross, the pope showed how God's heart is overwhelmed with grief at the thought of rejecting humanity, even though humanity has rejected him. The passage he refers to is Hosea 11:1–8.

> *What more could he do for us that he has not done? He has opened his very Heart to us, as the most secret chamber wherein to lead our soul, his chosen spouse.*
>
> **John Tauler**

When Israel was a child I loved him,
    out of Egypt I called my son.
The more I called them,
    the further they went from me,
Sacrificing to the Baals
    and burning incense to idols.
Yet it was I who taught Ephraim to walk,
    who took them in my arms;
I drew them with human cords,
    with bands of love;
I fostered them like one
    who raises an infant to his cheeks. . . .
How could I give you up, O Ephraim,
    or deliver you up, O Israel?
My heart is overwhelmed,
    my pity is stirred.

According to Pope Benedict, the word *overwhelmed* here is a much stronger expression than *broken*. He writes,

God's Heart turns around—here the Bible uses the same word as in the depiction of God's judgment on the sinful cities of Sodom and Gomorrah (Gn 19:25); the word expresses a total collapse: not one stone remains upon another. The same word is applied to the havoc wrought by love in God's Heart in favor of his people.

In all these writings of Pope Benedict, we see the devotion of God. It is from here that our devotion begins. The thought of rejecting his beloved so overwhelms the heart of God that he chooses to sacrifice himself for the beloved. When humanity rejected God and his plan for a loving union with humanity—a union which because it was loving needed to be freely accepted and chosen by humanity (the party receiving God's proposal)—God did not give up on humanity. God was too devoted to us. So God devised a new plan. God sent his Son, the Second Person of the Eternal Communion of Love known as the Most Holy Trinity, to become one with us. Though humanity rejected God's offer of loving union, God, knowing that our ultimate happiness depended upon such a union, set out to prove his love in a new and wonderful way.

The Incarnation

In his *Spiritual Exercises*, St. Ignatius of Loyola would have us imagine the Holy Trinity in the glory of heaven, looking over the world with loving eyes. He invites us to see

> how the three Divine Persons gazed on the whole surface or circuit of the world, full of people; and how, seeing that they were all going down into hell, they decide in their eternity that the Second Person should become a human being, in order to save the human race. And thus, when the fullness of time had come, they sent the angel St. Gabriel to Our Lady.

Imagine that moment. God's passionate desire for union with humanity leads him to speak through an angel to Mary. While our

ancestral parents and humans ever since have rejected God's love
and plan, Mary said "yes" to it. She surrendered to a loving union
with God, and the Holy Spirit overshadowed her. At that moment
a new human life, the likes of which the world had never seen nor
will ever see again, was conceived. St. Augustine and other Fathers of
the Church liked to say that Mary first received the Word into her
Immaculate Heart and then conceived the Word in her womb. In this
new person were joined two natures—human and divine. The loving union of God with humanity had begun in a new and wonderful
way, making possible every person's union with God. He took flesh
so that he could give his flesh to save humanity and to unite his flesh
with ours. The Second Vatican Council's *Constitution on the Church*
(*Lumen Gentium*) states, "By his incarnation, he, the Son of God, has
in a certain way united himself with each man" (*LG*, 22).

Cell by cell, the Second Person of the Blessed Trinity, now uniting
himself to our nature and our flesh, began to develop in the womb
of his mother. Within twenty-one days his first organ appeared. His
tiny physical heart began to beat under the heart of his mother. Over
nine months he grew and developed as every baby does until at last
he was born.

We know the story. His parents, Mary and Joseph, had to leave
Galilee and go to Judea to register in a census that required all people
to return to their ancestral homes. In a prophetic anticipation of further developments to God's plan for loving union with humanity, the
baby is born in Bethlehem, a town whose very name means "House
of Bread." Jesus, who would one day declare, "I am the bread of life,"
(Jn 6:48) was born in a town that means bread. And where does his
mother place him? In a manger, a feeding trough.

Jesus is the Son of God made flesh who reveals the Father's love
in his every thought, word, and deed. As St. Peter put it immediately
after receiving the Holy Spirit at Pentecost,

> Jesus the Nazorean was a man commended to you by God
> with mighty deeds, wonders, and signs, which God worked
> through him in your midst, as you yourselves know. This
> man, delivered up by the set plan and foreknowledge of

God, you killed, using lawless men to crucify him. But God raised him up, releasing him from the throes of death, because it was impossible for him to be held by it. (Acts 2:22–24)

His entire life on earth was a revelation of the love of God, the love that is both eros and agape. This love reached its climax, its fullest expression, on the cross where he suffered and died. As St. Paul wrote, "God proves his love for us in that while we were still sinners Christ died for us" (Rom 5:8).

The Eucharist

Before Jesus died, he ate the Passover meal with his disciples and transformed it into a New Passover, a meal of the New Covenant in which God would unite himself to humanity in a new and wonderful way. In his final homily at the 2005 World Youth Day in Cologne, Pope Benedict talked about the Last Supper and the transformation that occurred there and that continues in every celebration of the Eucharist. He said,

> What is happening? How can Jesus distribute his Body and his Blood? By making the bread into his Body and the wine into his Blood, he anticipates his death, he accepts it in his heart, and he transforms it into an action of love. What on the outside is simply brutal violence—the Crucifixion— from within becomes an act of total self-giving love. This is the substantial transformation which was accomplished at the Last Supper and was destined to set in motion a series of transformations leading ultimately to the transformation of the world when God will be all in all.
>
> This first fundamental transformation of violence into love, of death into life, brings other changes in its wake. Bread and wine become his Body and Blood. But it must not stop there; on the contrary, the process of transformation must now gather momentum. The Body and Blood of Christ are given to us so that we ourselves will be

transformed in our turn. We are to become the Body of Christ, his own flesh and blood. (cf. 1 Cor 15:28; Homily, August 21, 2005)

Again we see God's eros and agape coming together in Jesus. God created humanity for love and love desires union with the beloved. His passionate desire for this union with humanity led Jesus to take bread and wine and to transform them into his own flesh and blood so that he might give himself to us in such a way that we could be one with him.

In his Letter to the Ephesians, St. Paul wrote about this intimate union of Jesus and his Body the Church (and by extension, each individual part of that Body). After advising husbands and wives about how they are to care for one another and sacrifice for one another, Paul quotes from the Book of Genesis, "For this reason a man shall leave [his] father and [his] mother and be joined to his wife, and the two shall become one flesh." Then Paul writes, "This is a great mystery, but I speak in reference to Christ and the church" (Eph 5:31–32).

> *The Pauline image of marriage, inscribed in the "great mystery" of Christ and the Church, brings together the redemptive dimension of love with its spousal dimension. In some sense it unites these two dimensions in a single one.*
>
> **Blessed John Paul II**

If Paul were here today, we'd be tempted to ask, "Are you talking about marriage or Christ's relationship to the Church?" And his answer would be, "yes." Paul is talking about a great mystery: how marriage is a sign of the intimate union that God desires with humanity. That is the reason marriage is sacred; it reveals something of the love of God, the communion that is the Holy Trinity.

The total self-offering of Jesus is made present in every celebration of the Mass and he gives himself to us in Holy Communion so that God's plan for union with us would be realized.

That's the True Love Story, the story of God who is so completely devoted to his beloved human creatures that he won't give up on us.

It's a story that is not over but continues throughout history. While the revelation of this love is complete, it is expressed from time to time in new ways to new generations, all because God continues to communicate the devotion and love of his heart to people of all times. Our love story continues in the next chapter.

Prayer Exercise: The Litany of the Sacred Heart of Jesus

The Litany of the Sacred Heart of Jesus is one of the most beautiful and profound prayers of the Church. Its invocations are rich in scriptural allusions and theology, and many recall the writings of St. Margaret Mary. In 1899, Pope Leo XIII approved the litany in its present form, with thirty-three invocations in honor of the thirty-three years of Jesus' earthly life.

Blessed John Paul II said, "This prayer, recited and meditated, becomes a true school of the interior life, the school of the Christian" because "in the Heart of Christ there is a synthesis of all the mysteries of our faith" (Angelus Messages, June 27, 1982, and July 1, 1984). The litany is suitable for both individual and group prayer.

To enter more deeply into the litany, we present the thirty-three invocations of the Sacred Heart Litany with related passages of scripture.

Let us meditate on the depths of the Sacred Heart of Jesus.
Lord, have mercy on us.
Christ, have mercy.
Lord, have mercy on us. Christ, hear us.
Christ, graciously hear us.
God, the Father of heaven,
Have mercy on us. *(Repeat this response after each invocation below.)*
God, the Son, Redeemer of the world . . .
God, the Holy Spirit . . .
Holy Trinity, one God . . .

Heart of Jesus, Son of the eternal Father, have mercy on us.
> John 8:52–59 "Before Abraham came to be, I AM."
> John 14:8–10 "Whoever has seen me has seen the Father."

Heart of Jesus, formed by the Holy Spirit in the womb of the Virgin Mary, have mercy on us.
> Luke 1:26–45 "The Holy Spirit will come upon you."
> Psalm 139:13–15 "You knit me in my mother's womb. . . . I am fearfully, wonderfully made."

Heart of Jesus, substantially united to the Word of God, have mercy on us.
> John 1:1–5 "In the beginning was the Word . . . and the Word was God."
> Hebrews 1:1–4 "In these last days God spoke to us through a Son."

Heart of Jesus, of infinite majesty, have mercy on us.
> 1 Chronicles 29:10–13 "Yours, O Lord, are grandeur and power, majesty, splendor, and glory."
> Daniel 7:9–14 "One like a son of man . . . received dominion, glory, and kingship."

Heart of Jesus, sacred temple of God, have mercy on us.
> John 2:13–22 "Destroy this temple and in three days I will raise it up."
> Revelation 21:1–24 "I saw no temple in the city, for its temple is the Lord God almighty and the Lamb."

Heart of Jesus, tabernacle of the Most High, have mercy on us.
> John 1:14 "And the Word became flesh and made his dwelling among us."
> Hebrews 9:11–14 "Christ came passing through the greater and more perfect tabernacle not made by hands."

Heart of Jesus, house of God and gate of heaven, have mercy on us.
   Genesis 28:10–19 "This is nothing else but an abode of God,
      and that is the gateway to heaven!"
   John 1:43–51 "You will see the sky opened and the angels of
      God ascending and descending on the Son of Man."

Heart of Jesus, burning furnace of charity, have mercy on us.
   Song of Songs 8:6–8 Love's "flames are a blazing fire. Deep
      waters cannot quench love."
   Hebrews 12:28–29 "Our God is a consuming fire."

Heart of Jesus, abode of justice and love, have mercy on us.
   Psalm 9 "It is God who judges the world with justice."
   Romans 3:23–26 "They are justified freely by his grace."

Heart of Jesus, full of goodness and love, have mercy on us.
   Romans 5 "God proves his love for us in that while we were still
      sinners Christ died for us."
   1 John 4:9–19 "Perfect love drives out fear."

Heart of Jesus, abyss of all virtues, have mercy on us.
   1 Corinthians 2:9–16 "We have the mind of Christ."
   Colossians 3:12–17 "Over all these put on love, the bond of
      perfection."

Heart of Jesus, most worthy of all praise, have mercy on us.
   Revelation 5:6–14 "Worthy is the Lamb to receive honor and
      glory and blessing."
   Psalm 136 "Praise the Lord, who is so good; God's love endures
      forever."

Heart of Jesus, king and center of all hearts, have mercy on us.
   Psalms 98 and 99 "The Lord is king; let the earth rejoice."
   John 18:33–38 "My kingdom does not belong to this world."

Heart of Jesus, in whom are all the treasures of wisdom and knowledge, have mercy on us.

> Colossians 2:1–8 "Christ, in whom are hidden all the treasures of wisdom and knowledge."
>
> 1 Corinthians 1:18–25 "The foolishness of God is wiser than human wisdom."

Heart of Jesus, in whom dwells the fullness of divinity, have mercy on us.

> Colossians 2:9–10 "In him dwells the whole fullness of the deity bodily."
>
> Colossians 1:15–20 "In him all the fullness was pleased to dwell."

Heart of Jesus, in whom the Father was well pleased, have mercy on us.

> Matthew 3:13–17 "This is my beloved Son, with whom I am well pleased."
>
> Matthew 17:1–8 "This is my beloved Son, with whom I am well pleased. Listen to him."

Heart of Jesus, of whose fullness we have all received, have mercy on us.

> John 1:16–18 "From his fullness we have all received."
>
> Ephesians 3:14–21 "That you may be filled with the fullness of God."

Heart of Jesus, desire of the everlasting hills, have mercy on us.

> Genesis 49:22–26 "The blessings of the everlasting mountains, the delights of the eternal hills."
>
> Psalm 121 "I raise my eyes toward the mountains."

Heart of Jesus, patient and most merciful, have mercy on us.

> Psalm 145 "The Lord is gracious and merciful, slow to anger and abounding in love."
>
> 2 Peter 3:8–9 "He is patient with you, not wishing that any should perish."

Heart of Jesus, generous to all who turn to you, have mercy on us.
>   Romans 10:11–13 "The same Lord is Lord of all, enriching all
>   who call upon him."
>   2 Corinthians 8:9 "For your sake Jesus became poor although
>   he was rich, so that by his poverty you might become rich."

Heart of Jesus, fountain of life and holiness, have mercy on us.
>   John 4:4–41 "The water that I shall give will become a spring
>   of water welling up to eternal life."
>   John 7:37–39 "Let anyone who thirsts come to me and drink.
>   . . . Rivers of living water will flow from within him."

Heart of Jesus, propitiation for our sins, have mercy on us.
>   Hebrews 9 "Once for all he has appeared to take away sin by
>   his sacrifice."
>   1 John 2:1–2 "He is expiation for our sins and those of the
>   whole world."

Heart of Jesus, loaded down with opprobrium, have mercy on us.
>   Galatians 3:13–14 "Christ ransomed us by becoming a curse
>   for us."
>   Luke 23:33–43 "Even the soldier jeered at him."

Heart of Jesus, bruised for our offenses, have mercy on us.
>   Isaiah 52:13–54:12 "He was crushed for our sins."
>   Matthew 27:26–31 "Weaving a crown out of thorns, they placed
>   it on his head."

Heart of Jesus, obedient to death, have mercy on us.
>   Philippians 2:6–11 "He humbled himself, becoming obedient
>   to death, even death on a cross."
>   Hebrews 5:1–10 "He learned obedience from what he suffered."

Heart of Jesus, pierced with a lance, have mercy on us.
>   John 19:31–37 "One soldier thrust his lance into his side and
>   immediately blood and water flowed out."

Zechariah 12:10 "They shall look on him whom they have thrust through, and they shall mourn for him as one mourns for an only son."

Heart of Jesus, source of all consolation, have mercy on us.
2 Corinthians 1:3–7 "Blessed be the God of all encouragement."
Isaiah 66:10–13 "As a mother comforts her son, so shall I comfort you."

Heart of Jesus, our life and resurrection, have mercy on us.
John 11:1–44 "I am the resurrection and the life."
Colossians 1:18 "He is the beginning, the firstborn from the dead."

Heart of Jesus, our peace and reconciliation, have mercy on us.
John 20:19–23 "Peace be with you."
Ephesians 1:3–10 "He set forth a plan to sum up all things in Christ, in heaven and on earth."

Heart of Jesus, victim for our sins, have mercy on us.
Matthew 26:26–29 "This is my blood of the covenant that will be shed on behalf of many for the forgiveness of sins."
1 Peter 2:22–25 "He bore our sins in his body upon the cross."

Heart of Jesus, salvation of all who trust in you, have mercy on us.
Acts 4:5–12 "There is no salvation through anyone else, nor is there any other name under heaven by which we are to be saved."
Psalm 56 "In you I trust, I do not fear."

Heart of Jesus, hope of those who die in you, have mercy on us.
John 14:1–3 "I am going to prepare a place for you."
Romans 8:28–39 "What will separate us from the love of Christ?"

Heart of Jesus, delight of all the saints, have mercy on us.
>Psalm 16 "You will show me the path to life, abounding joy in your presence, the delights at your right hand forever."
>Revelation 7:9–17 "God will wipe away every tear from their eyes."

Lamb of God, who takes away the sins of the world,
Spare us, O Lord.
Lamb of God, who takes away the sins of the world,
Graciously hear us, O Lord.
Lamb of God, who takes away the sins of the world,
Have mercy on us, O Lord.

Jesus, meek and humble of heart,
Make our hearts like Yours.

Let us pray.
Almighty and eternal God, look upon the pierced Heart of Your most beloved Son and upon the praises and satisfaction which He offers You for the salvation of sinners. In Your great goodness, grant us forgiveness and the things we ask in the name of our Lord Jesus Christ, who lives and reigns with You forever and ever. Amen.

3 / The True Love Story Continues

The Gospel of John begins, "In the beginning was the Word, and the Word was with God, and the Word was God" (Jn 1:1). Fourteen verses later we read, "And the Word became flesh" (Jn 1:14). Jesus is the Word-Made-Flesh and as such he is God's perfect communication to us. Everything that God wanted us to know about himself, he communicated to us through Jesus. The Letter to the Hebrews makes this very clear, beginning with these words, "In times past, God spoke in partial and various ways to our ancestors through the prophets; in these last days, he spoke to us through a son" (Heb 1:1).

Revelation

There is no new revelation after Jesus. The Second Vatican Council said in its constitution *Divine Revelation* (*Dei Verbum*) that Jesus "completed and perfected Revelation" (*DV,* 4). The *Catechism* states that "Christ, the Son of God made man, is the Father's one, perfect and unsurpassable Word. In him he has said everything; there will be no other word than this one" (*CCC,* 65).

What are we to make, then, of the many appearances of our Lord to the saints throughout history? Aren't these new revelations? And, specific to our topic, what are we to make of the various apparitions of the Sacred Heart and of the various ways that devotion to the Heart of Christ have been expressed throughout history?

The *Catechism* tells us, "Yet even if Revelation is already complete, it has not been made completely explicit; it remains for Christian faith gradually to grasp its full significance over the course of the centuries" (*CCC,* 66). In the first place, for example, the perfect communication of God needs to be translated into the languages of different peoples and proclaimed to the ends of the earth.

Jesus told the apostles that they would gradually grasp the significance of what he revealed to them. At the Last Supper, he said that they wouldn't be able to understand everything that he had told them. But he reassured them that after he departed, he would send the Holy Spirit to help them understand what he had revealed. "I have much more to tell you, but you cannot bear it now. But when he comes, the Spirit of truth, he will guide you to all truth" (Jn 16:12–13).

So this is the way we understand the development of Sacred Heart devotion. Over the centuries, Jesus has sent his Spirit to help the Church to understand better the revelation of his love. Jesus himself has appeared to various individuals to speak to them about the love that he revealed definitively on the cross. Moreover, he has revealed his love through apparitions of a universal symbol for love—the heart, his heart.

Jesus Appears to Saul

The first recorded appearance of Jesus after he ascended to heaven can be found in the Acts of the Apostles. A devout Jew named Saul was on his way from Jerusalem to Damascus with letters authorizing him to apprehend "any men or women who belonged to the Way." On the road, "a light from the sky suddenly flashed around him," blinding him. From the light came a voice that asked, "Saul, Saul, why are you persecuting me?" When Saul asked him to identify himself, the voice responded, "I am Jesus, whom you are persecuting" (Acts 9:1–9).

> *As a body is one though it has many parts, and all the parts of the body, though many, are one body, so also Christ.*
>
> **1 Corinthians 12:12**

In that very sentence, the revelation of Jesus becomes more explicit. It makes clear that Jesus is one with his followers. Jesus didn't ask, "Saul, why are you persecuting my Church?" He asked him, "Why are you persecuting me?" Jesus is one with his followers. He is the head and his followers are the body. Years later, as an apostle and letter writer, Paul would explain this revelation of Jesus in several places, most notably 1 Corinthians 12.

What Jesus told Paul on the road to Damascus was not a new revelation, but it further explained something that had been revealed at the Last Supper. On that night Jesus taught his apostles that he was giving them his Body and Blood so that they might eat and be one with him.

> Remain in me, as I remain in you. Just as a branch cannot bear fruit on its own unless it remains on the vine, so neither can you unless you remain in me. I am the vine, you are the branches. Whoever remains in me and I in him will bear much fruit, because without me you can do nothing. (Jn 15:4–5)

Through the Eucharist, which was instituted at the Last Supper, Jesus is one with his followers.

Fathers of the Church

Jesus' blinding appearance to Paul is a continuation of the True Love Story, a further teaching designed to help people better understand the definitive revelation of Jesus. Centuries later there would be more recorded apparitions. But in the first millennium of the Church, the Holy Spirit worked quietly in the minds and hearts of the faithful to develop devotion to the Sacred Heart of Jesus.

Under the guidance of the Holy Spirit, five themes emerge in the writings of the saints and theologians of the first millennium.

1. The wounds of Jesus
2. Spiritual water
3. St. John at the Last Supper
4. Jesus as spouse
5. Consoling the Heart of Christ

The Wounds of Jesus

In the early Church and throughout the medieval period, there developed a devotion to the wounds of Jesus, in particular to the wound in his side. From the pierced side and heart of Jesus came blood and water, and, symbolically, the Church. As early as the beginning of the third century, the faithful paused at the three o'clock hour to reflect on the death of Jesus and the piercing of his side. St. Bernard (1070–1153) summed up the development of this devotion.

> The secret of his heart is laid bare in the wounds of his body. One can easily read in them the mystery of God's infinite goodness and merciful tenderness which came down to us like a dawning from on high. How could you indeed, Lord, show us more clearly than by your wounds that you are indeed "full of goodness and mercy abounding in love."

By the fourteenth century there were specific liturgical celebrations or Masses approved in honor of the five wounds of Jesus and the lance, which according to tradition the centurion Longinus thrust into the side of Jesus. In scripture we read, "One soldier thrust his lance into his side, and immediately blood and water flowed out" (Jn 19:34). The blood and water (pericardial fluid) that came from the pierced Heart of Jesus were seen in the early Church as symbols of the sacraments of the Eucharist and Baptism. St. John Chrysostom (d. 407) wrote,

> the Gospel relates that when Christ had died and was still hanging on the cross, the soldier approached him and pierced his side with the spear, and at once there came out water and blood. The one was a symbol of Baptism, the other of the [eucharistic] mysteries.

The pierced side of Christ on the cross reminded the early Church of the biblical account of the creation of Eve. "So the Lord God cast a deep sleep on the man, and while he was asleep, he took out one of his ribs and closed up its place with flesh. The Lord God then built up into a woman the rib that he had taken from the man" (Gn 2:21–22). Commenting on this scripture, Tertullian (160–235) wrote, "If Adam is a type of Christ then Adam's sleep is a symbol of the death of Christ, and by the wound in the side of Christ was formed the Church, the true Mother of all the living." St. Augustine (354–430) made explicit the connections between the blood and water, the sacraments, and the birth of the Church. "Adam sleeps that Eve may be born, Christ dies that the Church may be born. While Adam sleeps, Eve is formed from his side. When Christ is dead, his side is smitten with a spear, that thence may flow sacraments to form the Church." The devotion to the wounds of Christ is also present in the early eastern Church, as in the writings of St. John Chrysostom.

> *As God took the rib out of Adam's side and from it formed the woman, so Christ gives us water and blood from his wounded side and forms from it the Church . . . there the slumber of Adam, here the death-sleep of Jesus.*
>
> **St. John Chrysostom**

Spiritual Water

A second theme emerged in the early Church, the deeper understanding of the living water Jesus promised.

> On the last and greatest day of the feast, Jesus stood up and exclaimed, "Let anyone who thirsts come to me and drink. Whoever believes in me, as scripture says: 'Rivers of living water will flow from within him.'" He said this in reference to the Spirit that those who came to believe in him were to receive. (Jn 7:37–39)

Scholars debate whether Jesus is referring to himself or to the believer in this passage. Nor can we identify the literal source of the scripture Jesus quotes. But Jesus spoke these words about the "living water" during the Feast of Tabernacles, the commemoration of one of the miracles that occurred after Israel's exodus from Egypt (see Ex 17:1–7). In the desert the Israelites complained of thirst, so Moses struck a rock with his staff. Water gushed forth. The Jewish liturgy for this feast would have included prayers for rain and readings from passages of the Hebrew scriptures about abundant water (Ez 47:1ff. and Zec 14:8).

St. Paul was the first to equate Christ with the rock in the desert that produced abundant water. He wrote, "They drank from a spiritual rock that followed them, and the rock was the Christ" (1 Cor 10:4).

Water from the side of Christ, wash me. Passion of Christ, strengthen me.

Attributed to St. Ignatius of Loyola

Like the theme of the wounds of Christ, the theme of spiritual water sees the water from the side of Christ as the origin of baptismal grace (and the Church). In the earliest reference to the Heart of Christ after the New Testament, we find St. Justin (100–163) writing, "We Christians are the true Israel which springs from Christ, for we are drawn out of his heart as out of a rock."

A little later, St. Irenaeus (d. 202) shows how the water that comes from the side of Christ represents the Holy Spirit.

The Church is the fountain of living water that flows to us from the Heart of Christ. Where the Church is, there is the Spirit of God, and where the Spirit of God is, there is the Church and all grace. He who has no part in this Spirit will receive no nourishment or life at the breast of our mother Church, nor can he drink of the crystal-clear spring which issues from the Body of Christ.

This Spirit now dwells in the baptized, forming the Church. Thus the words of Jesus declaring that "rivers of living water will flow from within him" can be taken to mean both from within Jesus, who gives the Spirit as a gift from his very heart pierced on the cross, and from within the believer, who receives this gift in Baptism.

St. Cyprian (d. 258) adds a further scripture to this theme, "All you who are thirsty, come to the water!" (Is 55:1). Reflecting on this verse in the light of St. Paul and the Gospel of John, St. Cyprian writes,

If people thirst, says Isaiah, then God will give them water in the desert. He will make it spring for them from the rock; for the rock will be split and water will flow and my people will drink. This is fulfilled in the Gospel when Christ, who is the true rock, was split by the thrust of the lance in his painful death. Alluding to the prediction of the prophet, he cried: If any man thirst, let him come, and let him drink who believes in me. As the scripture says: Streams of living water shall issue from his body.

You can see the pattern here. Gradually, under the gentle guidance of the Holy Spirit, the Church grew in its understanding of the significance of the water and the blood that gushed forth from Jesus' pierced side as he hung on the cross. And the themes that continued to emerge led to our devotion to the Heart of Christ.

St. John at the Last Supper

Let's consider a powerful third theme, the Apostle John laying his head on the chest of Jesus at the Last Supper. In John's gospel we read how "the disciple whom Jesus loved" (identified with John himself) lays his head on Jesus' chest. According to the gospel account, he did so under the direction of Peter who wanted him to find out from Jesus the identity of his betrayer.

But the early Church saw the image of John reclining on Jesus' breast as a spiritual symbol of the Church itself. As John drew near to the Heart of Jesus, so the Church is called to draw near to her Lord. There the Church will learn the secrets of his heart. There the Church will find wisdom and courage. Perhaps because John drew near to the Heart of Jesus at the Last Supper, he was the only apostle with the strength to stand under the cross the next day. The knowledge of the love of the Heart of Jesus gave him that strength. Moreover, from the Heart of Jesus John received wisdom about God's love that was later communicated in the high theology of his gospel and his three letters.

> *Because in Jesus' breast are hidden all the treasures of wisdom and knowledge, it was fitting that the one who leaned upon his breast was the one to whom he had granted a larger gift of unique wisdom and knowledge than to the rest.*
>
> **St. Bede the Venerable**

St. Augustine (354–430) grasped that John's wisdom was a gift from Christ's Heart.

> Among his fellows and collaborators, the other evangelists, John received from our Lord (on whose breast he lay at the Last Supper, in order thereby to signify that he drew loftier mysteries from his inmost Heart) the special and peculiar gift that he should say such things of the Son of God as would stimulate, without satisfying, the spirits of little ones, who are still incapable of comprehension; but for the more mature who have reached the adult state, these same words serve to exercise and nourish their souls.

St. Augustine's contemporary, St. Paulinus of Nola (d. 431) spoke of it eloquently. "John, who rested blissfully on the breast of our Lord, was inebriated with the Holy Spirit who searches even the deep things of God; from the Heart of all-creating Wisdom, he quaffed an understanding which transcends that of any creature."

Jesus as Spouse

The fourth biblical theme that led the early Church into devotion to the Heart of Christ is the recognition of the deep, intimate love of Christ for the Church and for the individual believer.

It starts in the Song of Songs, a short book in the Old Testament that consists of erotic poetry and makes no mention of God. Does Song of Songs, also known as Song of Solomon or Canticle of Canticles, belong in the Bible? As we've seen, erotic love, though wounded by sin, is an image of the eros of God. The Hebrew scriptures teem with references to the love of God for his people, even comparing God's love for Israel to the love of a husband for his unfaithful wife. Seeing itself as the new Israel, the Church saw in the poetry of Song of Songs the passionate expression of Christ's love for his Church—and his particular love for each individual person. In this passage, the lover addresses his beloved. "Arise, my beloved, my beautiful one, and come! 'O my dove in the clefts of the rock,' in the secret recesses of the cliff, let me see you, let me hear your voice, for your voice is sweet, and you are lovely" (Sg 2:13–14).

Pope St. Gregory the Great (540–604), in his commentary on the Song of Songs, leads our understanding of these verses.

> *It seems as if God is crying out to us: "My heart is restless until I may rest in you, my beloved creation."*
>
> **Henri Nouwen**

> Arise, my love, my sister, and come, my dove, in the clefts of the rock, in the hollow places in the wall. By the clefts of the rock I mean the wounds in the hands and feet of Christ hanging on the cross. By the hollow places in the wall I mean the wound in his side made by the lance. Like

the dove in the rock the simple soul finds in these wounds
the food that will strengthen her.

Once again the rock is an image of Christ. From the sensual imagery of the Song of Songs came the tender intimacy that is a part of traditional devotion to the Sacred Heart.

Consoling the Heart of Christ

The fifth theme that appears in the writings of the patristic era is the amazing idea of giving consolation to the Heart of Jesus.

The early Church reflected not only on the physical wounds of Jesus, but also on his interior sufferings, the deepest sufferings of his heart. St. Justin (100–163), commenting on Psalm 22, the psalm that prophesied the passion of Christ, wrote about the interior sufferings of Jesus.

> The words, "My heart is become like wax, melting in the midst of my bowels" (Ps 22:15), are a prediction of that which Jesus was to undergo in the night when they went out against him in the Garden of Olives in order to arrest him. For it is written in the memoirs of the apostles that his sweat ran down to the earth as drops of blood, and that his heart quaked and dissolved within him, in order that we may know that the Son, in accordance with the Father's will, really did endure this for our sakes, and that we might not imagine that as Son of God he had no feeling for all that happened and befell him.

A few centuries later, St. Hilary (315–367), writing about Psalm 69 that prophesied the sufferings of the Messiah, addressed the Lord's desire to be consoled in the midst of his sufferings. Hilary refers to the following verse: "Insult has broken my heart, and I am weak; I looked for compassion, but there was none, for comforters, but found none" (Ps 69:21). St. Hilary interprets this verse as Christ's longing for comfort from those he suffered for. "Ready to die for us, he was assailed by another wish reflected in the Psalms: 'I looked for someone to be

with me in my suffering and I found
no one.' He had come to save the lost
sheep of Israel, but he found no one to
console him and show him compassion in the midst of his anguish."

In Jesus Christ, who allowed
his heart to be pierced for us,
the true face of God is seen.

Pope Benedict XVI

Early Franciscans

Through these five themes, the Holy Spirit laid the foundation for
the full development of devotion to the Heart of Jesus that would
take place in the second millennium of the Church. That second
millennium of devotion to the Sacred Heart of Jesus began with the
Franciscans. St. Francis of Assisi (d. 1226) had a deep devotion to
both the physical wounds of Christ and to his interior sufferings, so
much so that he ultimately received the mystical gift of the stigmata,
the very wounds of Christ in his own body.

St. Francis's conversion occurred as he prayed before the crucifix
in the church of San Damiano, which, in the words of St. Bonaventure's biography of Francis, "was threatening to collapse." According
to Bonaventure, "while his tear-filled eyes were gazing at the Lord's
cross, he heard with his bodily ears a voice coming from the cross,
telling him three times: 'Francis, go and repair my house, which, as
you see, is falling completely into ruin.'" In time Francis came to
understand that this church building in need of repair was symbolic
of the Church, which had lost much of its early enthusiasm for the
gospel. From that time on, he lived and worked to return the Church
to its original simplicity and devotion in following Christ.

Toward the end of his life, as he meditated on the passion narrative
of the gospel, Francis, in the words of St. Bonaventure, "understood
that just as he had imitated Christ in the actions of his life, so he
should be conformed to him in the affliction and sorrow of his passion." Thus, while he was praying around the feast of the Exaltation
of the Cross, Francis had a vision of an angel, a six-winged Seraph,
and "between the wings the figure of a man crucified, with hands

and feet extended in the form of a cross and fastened to a cross." Francis felt sorrow for the crucified man and came to understand that "as Christ's lover, he might learn in advance that he was to be totally transformed into the likeness of Christ crucified, not by the martyrdom of his flesh, but by the fire of his love consuming his soul." This love imprinted on his body the mystical gift of the stigmata, the physical wounds of Jesus.

St. Bonaventure (d. 1274) himself wrote often about the Heart of Jesus. He wrote of his rapture at the union of his own heart with that of his king, brother, and friend.

> The heart I have found is the heart of my King and Lord, of my Brother and Friend, the most loving Jesus. I say without hesitation that his heart is also mine. Since Christ is my head, how could that which belongs to my head not also belong to me? As the eyes of my bodily head are truly my own, so also is the heart of my spiritual Head. Oh, what a blessed lot is mine to have one heart with Jesus! Having found this heart, both yours and mine, O most sweet Jesus, I will pray to you my God.

By following Jesus on the way of his Passion we not only see the Passion of Jesus, but we also see all the suffering in the world.

Pope Benedict XVI

Not only is St. Bonaventure's heart one with the Heart of Jesus, but also his heart is transformed, allowing him to pray to the Father with the thoughts and feelings of Jesus. As St. Paul wrote, "the Spirit too comes to the aid of our weakness; for we do not know how to pray as we ought, but the Spirit itself intercedes with inexpressible groanings"(Rom 8:26). The Holy Spirit is a gift right from the Heart of Jesus, so the Spirit transforms our hearts, helping us pray with the mind and Heart of Jesus.

Dominicans

While the early Franciscans promoted devotion to the wounds and Heart of Jesus, the Dominicans continued the theme of the Heart of Jesus as the source of wisdom, the sacraments, and the Church.

St. Albert the Great (d. 1280) wrote about the post-resurrection appearance of Jesus when he showed the apostles his wounded side. "Our Lord appeared to his disciples and showed them his side, in which rest all the riches of God's knowledge and wisdom; he showed his heart, which had already been wounded by his love for us before it was struck by the point of the lance." St. Albert sees here both the theme of wisdom and the theme of the interior suffering of the Heart of Jesus. It was Christ's passionate love for sinners that led to his Passion.

St. Albert extended our understanding of the Heart of Jesus as the source of the Church and its sacraments. "By the blood of his side and of his heart our Lord watered the garden of his Church, for with this blood he made the sacraments flow from his heart." St. Albert made a strong connection between the Heart of Jesus and the Eucharist, when he wrote, "In three ways did he espouse himself to the Church on the cross: through his blood; through the stretching out of his arms to embrace his bride in intimate love; and after his death through the opening of his side, from which the Church proceeded with the principal mysteries, the blood of redemption and the water of atonement."

The connection between the Heart of Jesus and the Eucharist strengthened as the Church entered the Middle Ages.

Mystics

The first appearance in which Jesus revealed his heart was recorded by a Benedictine Cistercian nun, St. Lutgard (d. 1246). Jesus first appeared to her when she was a lay woman of seventeen. He showed her the wound in his side. After entering the convent, St. Lutgard was given a special grace to be able to understand the psalms as they were sung in Latin, a language she had not learned. This was in response to her request for help in her prayer life. When she complained that this wasn't enough, Jesus appeared to her and asked her what she wanted. Her response was, "I want your heart!" To which Jesus responded, "And still more do I want yours!" What followed was a mystical exchange of hearts.

In 1370, St. Catherine of Siena, now a celebrated Doctor of the Church, experienced a similar gift in a vision in which her heart entered into the Heart of Jesus and his heart entered hers. This union of hearts led her to write this in a letter.

> Put your mouth at the heart of the Son of God, since it is a heart that casts the fire of charity and pours out blood to wash away your iniquities. I say that the soul that rests there and considers with the eye of the intellect the heart that is consumed and opened out of love, that soul receives in itself such conformity within, seeing itself so loved, that it cannot do anything but love.

In other words, the heart that intimately understands the love of the Heart of Jesus naturally wants to return love. Sharing in the passionate love of Christ, St. Catherine, like St. Francis, received the gift of the stigmata, though, in her humility, she asked that the marks of the wounds remain invisible. That request was granted.

The spirituality of the union of hearts can also be seen in three religious women of the Benedictine Cistercian monastery of Helfta: Mechthild of Magdeburg (1207–82), St. Mechthild of Hackeborn (1241–99), and St. Gertrude the Great (1256–1302). The prayers of St. Mechthild of Hackeborn to the Heart of Jesus were gathered into a book. The Jesuit saint, Peter Canisius (1521–1597), always carried this book with him, even to his deathbed. Writing in the third person, St. Mechthild described the union of hearts which she experienced with Jesus.

> She [Mechthild] saw how the Lord opened the wound of his sweet Heart, and said: "Behold the greatness of my love.

If you want to learn to know it, you will find it nowhere so clearly as in the words of the Gospel: 'As the Father has loved me, so have I loved you.'" The Lord united his sweet Heart with the soul's heart, bestowed on her all the graces of contemplation, devotion, and love, and made her rich in all good things.

In another place St. Mechthild wrote, "He made her rest tenderly on his heart and said: 'Take wholly my divine heart.' And the soul felt how the Godhead poured itself into her with mighty force like a stream."

It is near the Heart of Christ that man's heart is given the capacity of loving

Blessed John Paul II

This union of the devout soul to the Heart of Jesus is seen also in St. Gertrude, a confidante of St. Mechthild. St. Gertrude's *Spiritual Exercises* consists of seven days of meditations on the love of God. On the last day she writes,

> You have done such great and good things for me. . . . What shall I repay you for such unlimited good? What praise and thanksgiving could I offer to you even if I expended myself a thousand times? . . . Let me then offer you my entire soul that you have redeemed; let me confer upon you the love of my heart. Ah, may you transfer my life to you. May you carry me totally away in you and, enclosing me in you, make me one with you. . . . O heart that runs over with loving-kindness. O heart that overflows with charity. O heart that distills pleasantness. O heart full of compassion. . . . O dearest heart, I pray from my heart, absorb my heart totally in you. . . . O love, immerse my spirit in the flow of this mellifluous heart, burying in the depth of your divine mercy the total weight of my iniquity and thoughtlessness.

Other Figures

From this point, devotion to the Sacred Heart of Jesus tended to emphasize the union of the hearts of Christ and his followers.

The Carthusian order nurtured a devotion to the love of Christ revealed in his heart. In *The Life of Christ* by Ludolph of Saxony (d. 1378), we have the following reflection on the pierced Heart of Jesus. "The Heart of Christ was wounded for us with the wound of love, that through the opening of his side we may in return enter his Heart by means of love, and there be able to unite all our love with his divine love into one love, as the glowing iron is one with the fire."

St. Francis de Sales (1567–1622), who together with St. Jane Frances de Chantal founded the Visitation order of which St. Margaret Mary was a member, fostered devotion to the Heart of Christ, inviting believers to enter into the Heart of Jesus and see others with the love of Jesus.

> God's love is seated within the Savior's heart as on a royal throne. He beholds through the cleft of his pierced side all the hearts of the children of men. His heart is king of hearts, and he keeps his eyes fixed on our hearts. Just as those who peer through a lattice see clearly while they themselves are only half seen, so too the divine love within that heart, or rather that heart of divine love, always sees our hearts and looks on them with his eyes of love, while we do not see him, but only half see him.

St. Margaret Mary

Finally we come to St. Margaret Mary, the visionary who many think started the devotion to the Sacred Heart. But the survey we have just taken makes it clear that devotion to Christ's Heart has been present in the Church from its beginning.

On the feast of St. Francis of Assisi, October 4, 1673, Jesus spoke to the heart of St. Margaret Mary (1647–1690). He told her that he was giving her St. Francis to be her special patron in the coming days and years of trials. Why St. Francis? As her autobiography states, it was because of "his great love for the Passion of our Lord, a love which rendered him worthy of the sacred stigmata and made him one of the favorites of Jesus' heart."

A few months later, on December 27, the feast of St. John the Apostle, Jesus appeared to St. Margaret Mary as she prayed before the Blessed Sacrament. She described what happened in this way: "For a long time he kept me leaning on his breast, while he revealed the wonders of his love and the mysterious secrets of his Sacred Heart. Till then, he had always kept them hidden; but now, for the first time, he opened his Heart to me."

Margaret Mary described how Jesus revealed his heart as a heart on fire with love. "My divine Heart is so passionately fond of the human race, and of you in particular, that it cannot keep back the pent-up flames of its burning charity any longer. They must burst out through you and reveal my Heart to the world, so as to enrich mankind with my precious treasures." What followed was the uniting of Christ's Heart with her heart, transforming it. She described how it happened. "Next, he asked for my heart. I begged him to take it; he did, and placed it in his own divine Heart. He let me see it there—a tiny atom being completely burned up in that fiery furnace. Then, lifting it out—now a little heart-shaped flame—he put it back where he had found it."

This was the first of four appearances of Jesus to St. Margaret Mary. In the fourth or "Great Revelation," Jesus asked her to have a feast instituted in honor of his Sacred Heart. He said it was to be a feast of "reparation"—to make up for the coldness of most people toward his love, especially as revealed through the gift of the Eucharist. (Incidentally, this was not the first time that Jesus had asked for a feast. In 1206, Blessed Juliana of Liège (1193–1252) was asked by Christ to work for the institution of a feast in honor of his Body and Blood. This feast was to be the antidote for the coldness toward Christ's presence in the Eucharist. Pope Urban IV instituted the annual feast of

Corpus Christi in 1264, and he asked St. Thomas Aquinas to compose hymns for it.)

St. Margaret Mary's apparitions take us back to Paul. Remember how Jesus first appeared to Saul and revealed to him the truth that Jesus was one with his Church? From his conversion experience, St. Paul developed a theology of the Eucharist and the Body of Christ, which we find in his letters (esp. 1 Cor 11 and 12).

> *Our God is not a remote God, intangible in his blessedness. Our God has a heart.*
>
> **Pope Benedict XVI**

Through the efforts of her spiritual director, St. Claude de la Colombière (1641–82), St. Margaret Mary's visions were accepted as authentic by her superiors. But the Church moves very slowly when it comes to such revelations. It took a while to obtain approval for the feast of Jesus' Sacred Heart.

Papal Recognition

Though a feast in honor of the Sacred Heart had been celebrated in the fifteenth century in a Dominican house and though St. John Eudes (1601–1680) had composed fifteen different Mass texts for celebrating a feast in honor of the Sacred Heart, it wasn't until 1765 that an entire nation was given permission to celebrate such a feast. That nation was Poland. One by one, the bishops and people of other nations were also given permission, culminating in 1856 when the pope, Blessed Pius IX, placed the feast on the Church's liturgical calendar.

Blessed Pius IX's successor, Leo XIII (1810–1903), is perhaps best known for beginning the tradition of making explicit the Church's social teachings by writing the first social encyclical of the Church, *Rerum Novarum*. But he himself said that the "greatest act" of his pontificate was something else.

Leo XIII's "greatest act" is also part of our ongoing True Love Story, and it also involves a religious woman, a Good Shepherd Sister named Blessed Mary of the Divine Heart (1863–1899), who was beatified in 1975. In 1896, Jesus told Blessed Mary that though exterior devotion to his heart had been made official, he wanted "interior devotion." She understood him to mean that "He wished souls to get into the habit of uniting themselves more and more interiorly with him and of offering him their hearts as his abode." In 1898, Jesus asked her to write to Pope Leo requesting that he make a solemn act of consecration of the world to his Sacred Heart. After some hesitation and theological consultation, Pope Leo wrote the encyclical *Annum Sacrum* in which he called for this consecration to take place on the Sunday after the feast of the Sacred Heart, 1899. In the end, his act of consecration of the world to the Sacred Heart is what Pope Leo called "the greatest act of my pontificate."

> *Pure love is capable of great deeds. . . . It knows that only one thing is needed to please God: to do even the smallest things out of great love— love, and always love.*
>
> **St. Faustina Kowalska**

Pope Leo XIII shows us that an intimate relationship with Jesus that is expressed in devotion to his heart does not alienate one from social concerns. Rather, to enter more deeply into Jesus' heart leads us to share the desires of this heart so that humanity might know the love the Father has for all his children. It is this love that ultimately forms the basis for what Pope Paul VI called "the civilization of love," a term he first used on Pentecost Sunday, 1970.

St. Faustina

In the 1930s, Jesus appeared to St. Faustina Kowalska and requested a painting of himself with red and white rays emanating from his heart, and the words "Jesus, I trust in you" inscribed below. He also asked that the Sunday after Easter be celebrated as Divine Mercy Sunday to "proclaim that mercy is the greatest attribute of

God." The devotion that has come to be known as Divine Mercy is in no way in competition with the devotion to the Sacred Heart. St. Faustina's Divine Mercy devotion further developed and expressed the love of God symbolized in the Heart of Jesus from which gushed forth the sign of mercy for all humanity—the blood and water. We consider the Divine Mercy devotion at greater length in a later chapter.

Since Pope Leo XIII, every pope has encouraged devotion to the Sacred Heart of Jesus. Perhaps the most important document on the subject is Pope Pius XII's 1956 encyclical *On Devotion to the Sacred Heart* (*Haurietis Aquas*, Latin for "you shall draw waters"), presented on the centenary of the institution of the feast of the Sacred Heart for the universal Church. In this important encyclical, Pope Pius XII tells the True Love Story, the history of the love of the Heart of Christ as it appears in the scriptures and the Church's tradition, much as I have just done.

Our brief survey of devotion to the Heart of Jesus from its origins in the scriptures and through the lives and writings of the saints shows an increased appreciation for the mystery of God's passionate love revealed in the pierced side of Jesus on the cross.

In our next two chapters we see how devotion to the Sacred Heart is essentially eucharistic.

Prayer Exercise: Sacred Heart Prayers

Throughout history, the saints have expressed their love for the Sacred Heart of Jesus in beautiful prayers. Perhaps these examples will express what is in your heart.

St. Bernard (1090–1153)

O Heart of my supreme king! To you my heart pays homage joyfully. My pleasure consists in loving you, and it is my love which moves me to speak to you. What a charity must have urged you on, and yet, what pain must have tortured you when you exhausted yourself completely to give yourself to us and snatch us away from death! By the death which you endured for me, by your last heartbeat, O Heart so dear to me, I beseech you to accept my love, for I desire nothing else. Purify my heart so vain and hardened. Make it tender and watchful. Melt the ice of its lukewarmness. My heart is sinful: may your love penetrate its fibers. May it bring my heart wholly back to life. Wound it, O Jesus, with your own wound. Unite yourself with my heart, touch it, penetrate it with your grace.

St. Bonaventure (1221–1274)

O good Jesus, how beautiful and joyous a thing it is to dwell in your heart! It is the rich treasure, the precious pearl which we have uncovered, hidden in the secret of your pierced body, as in a dug-out field. O most gentle Jesus, I have found your heart, the heart of a king, the heart of a brother, the heart of a friend. Already your heart is my heart also. If you are my Head, Jesus, how can what belongs to the head not be called mine? See, O Jesus, you and I have one and the same heart.

St. Gertrude (1256–1302)

Hail! O Sacred Heart of Jesus, living and quickening source of eternal life, infinite treasure of the Divinity, and burning furnace of divine love. You are my refuge and my sanctuary, O my amiable Savior. Consume my heart with that burning fire with which yours is ever inflamed. Pour down on my soul those graces which flow from your love, and let my heart be so united with yours, that our wills may be one, and mine in all things, may be conformed to yours. May your divine will be equally the standard and rule of all my desires and of all my actions. Amen.

St. Catherine of Siena (1347–1380)

O charity, you are that sweet and holy bond that joins the soul to its creator; you bind God to man, and man to God. You give peace and put an end to war, you give patience, strength and long perseverance in every good and holy endeavor. You enlarge the heart that it may welcome friends and enemies and all creatures, because it is clothed with the affection of Jesus and follows him. O Christ, sweet Jesus, grant me this priceless favor of persevering for whoever possesses charity is founded on you, the living stone. He has learned from you how to love his Creator, by following your footsteps. In you I read the rule and the teaching that I must hold to, for you are the way, the truth, and the life; so by reading in you, who are the book of life, I shall be able to walk the straight path and attend only to the love of God and the salvation of my neighbor.

Bl. Marie of the Incarnation (1599–1672)

O eternal Father, through the Heart of Jesus, my way, my truth, and my life, I come to you. Through this heart I adore you for all those who do not adore you. I love you for all those who do not love you. I go in spirit through the whole world to seek for souls redeemed by the blood of Jesus. I embrace them in order to present them to you in his Sacred Heart, and in union with your merciful heart, I ask for their conversion.

St. John Eudes (1601–1681)

Father of mercies and God of all consolation, because of your great love for us you have given us the loving heart of your Son so that, together with him, we might love you perfectly as with one heart. Grant us, we pray, now that our hearts are united with each other and with the Heart of Jesus, that all we do may be performed out of love for him and that, through his intervention, all the right desires of our heart may be fulfilled.

St. Claude de la Colombière (1641–1682)

O God, what will you do to conquer the fearful hardness of our hearts? Lord, you must give us new hearts, tender hearts, sensitive hearts, to replace hearts that are made of marble and of bronze. You must give us your own heart, Jesus. Come, lovable Heart of Jesus. Place your heart deep in the center of our hearts and enkindle in each heart a flame of love as strong, as great, as the sum of all the reasons that I have for loving you, my God. O holy Heart of Jesus, dwell hidden in my heart, so that I may live only in you and only for you, so that, in the end, I may live with you eternally in heaven. Amen.

St. Margaret Mary (1647–1690)

I.

O eternal Father, permit me to offer you the Heart of Jesus Christ, your well-beloved Son, as he offers himself in sacrifice. Graciously receive this offering on my behalf and receive all the desires, all the sentiments, all the affections, all the movements, and all the acts of this Sacred Heart. They are all mine, since he immolates himself for me, and since I intend to have no other desires henceforth but his. Receive them in satisfaction for my sins, and in thanksgiving for all his benefits. Graciously receive, then, all the merits of the Sacred Heart of your divine Son which I offer, and grant me in return all the graces which are necessary for me, especially the grace of final perseverance. Receive them as so many acts of love, adoration, and praise which I offer to your Divine Majesty, since it is by your divine Son alone that you are worthily honored and glorified. Amen.

II.

O Sacred Heart of Jesus, I choose you as my only refuge. Be to me strength in conflict, the support of my weakness, a light and a guide in the darkness of this life, and finally atonement for all my faults and the sanctification of all my desires and actions. I unite mine with yours and offer them to you, in order that you may come to me to unite me to yourself. Amen.

III.

O most Sacred Heart of Jesus, you desire so ardently to shower your favors upon the unfortunate, and to teach those who want to advance in the school of your love; you continually invite me to be meek and humble of heart like you. For this reason you convince me that in order to gain your friendship and to become your true disciple, I can do nothing better than to try henceforth to be truly meek and humble. . . . O Jesus, permit me to enter your Heart as I would a school. In this school teach me the science of the saints, the science of pure love. O Good Master, I shall listen attentively to your words: "Learn of me for I am gentle and humble of heart, and you will find rest for your souls."

St. Madeleine Sophie Barat (1779–1865)

Sacred Heart of Jesus, my light, my love, and my life: lead me to know you and to love only you. May I live to you alone, in you, by you, and for you.

Bl. John Henry Newman (1801–1890)

O most sacred, most loving heart of Jesus, Thou art concealed in the Holy Eucharist, and Thou beatest for us still. Now as then Thou sayest, "With desire I have desired." I worship Thee, then, with all my best love and awe, with my fervent affection, with my most subdued, most resolved will. O make my heart beat with Thy heart. Purify it of all that is earthly, all that is proud and sensual, all that is hard and cruel, of all perversity, of all disorder, of all deadness. So fill it with Thee, that neither the events of the day nor the circumstances of the time may have power to ruffle it; but that in Thy love and Thy fear it may have peace.

Bl. John XXIII (1881–1963)

You are my kind Jesus, the gentle lamb who called me your friend, who looked with love upon me, a sinner, who blessed me when I cursed you, who prayed for me on the cross, and from your pierced heart let flow a stream of divine Blood that washed away my impurities and cleansed my soul of its sins; you snatched me from death by dying for me, and by conquering death you gave me life. You opened to me the gates of paradise. O the love of Jesus! And yet at last this love has conquered and I am with you, my Master, my Friend, my Spouse, my Father. Here I am in your heart! What then would you have me do?

Fr. Herbert F. Smith, S.J. (b. 1922)

O Jesus, love of you is the gift I beg from your heart. Your human heart wounded for love of me, burning with love, is the pattern of love to which I consecrate myself. My God, fill my heart with a passionate love for you that will move mountains and give all. Breathe into me a love worlds removed from sentimental love that gives nothing but sighs and does nothing but take. Let me sigh and long for you, O God, but let my love be more in action than in word. Jesus, I give you all I have and am and can obtain. Take my heart and give me yours that I may always live in you and you in me. Amen.

4 / Entering into the Heart of the Word

Devotion to the Sacred Heart is simply a relationship with Jesus Christ that grows ever more personal and deep. What is the best way to develop such a relationship? The answer is simple: through the Eucharist.

The Second Vatican Council reaffirmed in its *Constitution on the Church* that the Eucharist is "the source and summit of the Christian life" (*LG*, 11). It is in the Eucharist that we see most clearly God's devotion to humanity. It is in the Eucharist that we can best respond to God's devotion. In this chapter and the next we consider how the Eucharist leads to and feeds our devotion to the Sacred Heart of Jesus. The Eucharist is the Mass, a celebration that consists of two parts. First we look at the Liturgy of the Word and then at the Liturgy of the Eucharist.

Christ, the Word of God

According to the Vatican II *Constitution on the Sacred Liturgy* (*Sacrosanctum Concilium*), Christ "is present in his word since it is he himself who speaks when the holy scriptures are read in the Church" (*SC,* 7). When the scriptures are proclaimed during the Eucharist, Jesus is present, speaking to us. But he is also present speaking to us whenever we open the scriptures and prayerfully read them. Christ speaks to us with the Father and in the Holy Spirit through the word of God, written or spoken. As the Vatican II document on *Divine Revelation* states,

> In the sacred books, the Father who is in heaven meets His children with great love and speaks with them; and the force and power in the word of God is so great that it stands as the support and energy of the Church, the strength of faith for her sons, the food of the soul, the pure and everlasting source of spiritual life. (*DV,* 21)

Christ is present in the Word. He is the "living and active" Word (Heb 4:12). He is God's perfect communication to humanity, revealing to us who God is and what it means to be human. Thus scripture reading is unlike any other kind of reading. We've all heard the teachings and stories of the Bible before, and we don't read the scriptures for new information. Rather, we prayerfully read the scriptures in order to meet Christ and grow in our relationship with him.

Pope Benedict has been clear about the power of scripture to deepen our relationship with Christ. After the 2008 Synod of Bishops, in his apostolic exhortation entitled *Word of the Lord* (*Verbum Domini*), Pope Benedict used the words *encounter* and *relationship* dozens of times. He wrote,

> The Christian life is essentially marked by an encounter with Jesus Christ, who calls us to follow him. . . . With the Synod Fathers I express my heartfelt hope for the flowering of "a new season of greater love for sacred Scripture on the part of every member of the People of God, so that their prayerful and faith-filled reading of the Bible will,

with time, deepen their personal relationship with Jesus."
(*VD*, 72)

Calling for a "deepening relationship with the divine word," Pope Benedict made it clear that our spirituality—our understanding of God's devotion to us and our response to that devotion—must be grounded in scripture. "We must never forget that all authentic and living Christian spirituality is based on *the word of God proclaimed, accepted, celebrated and meditated upon in the Church*" (*VD*, 121). Whether through personal prayer with the Bible or the proclamation of the Word in the Liturgy, we meet the Word-Made-Flesh and encounter the Heart of Jesus in the scriptures.

To know someone personally (and not just know *about* that person), you have to spend time with him or her. You must listen. The disciples grew in their relationship with Jesus by spending time with him, observing his actions, and listening to his words. We do the same when we spend quality time with Jesus in the Word. He not only teaches us and forms our attitudes and values, but also he shares himself with us. Pope Benedict made abundantly clear in his first encyclical that "being Christian is not the result of an ethical choice or a lofty idea, but the encounter with an event, a person, which gives life a new horizon and a definitive direction" (*DCE*, 1). Because our values and principles, our thoughts and attitudes, are formed by our relationships, it's only through our relationship with Christ that we may become Christians.

How could one live without the knowledge of Scripture, by which we come to know Christ himself, who is the life of believers?

St. Jerome

By spending time together, Jesus and his apostles became close. They followed him, watching and listening. What do Jesus' contemporary followers do to get close to him? Do they read the Bible? According to recent surveys, 87 percent of Catholics interviewed said they had a Bible in their homes. That's good news. Now the bad news: 32 percent said that they never read it, and 31 percent said they read it a few times a year. Only 8 percent said they read it daily. Another survey, this time of all Christians, indicated that the average Christian spends more time in one evening watching television than the whole rest of the week reading the Bible. What's forming the attitudes and values of the average Christian? What's entering into the imagination of the average Christian? Obviously we are being formed more by the world and its values and images than by Christ "living and active" in the Word.

> *Whatever is true, whatever is honorable, whatever is just, whatever is pure, whatever is lovely, whatever is gracious, if there is any excellence and if there is anything worthy of praise, think about these things.*
>
> **Philippians 4:8–9**

Jesus called twelve to be his apostles. They spent much time with him and through his words and actions he formed them. They grew in a deep relationship with him. They grew in their knowledge of his love for them, his devotion to them, and they in turn grew in their loving devotion to him. He called his apostles "friends" (see Jn 15:15), and he calls us to be the same. Friends know the intimate secrets of the heart of one another. So it is with Jesus who desires to share with us the secrets of his heart. He does so through the scriptures.

Speaking about St. Paul's encounter with Christ on the way to Damascus, Pope Benedict said,

> we are only Christians if we encounter Christ. Of course, he does not show himself to us in this overwhelming, luminous way, as he did to Paul to make him the Apostle to all peoples. But we too can encounter Christ in reading Sacred Scripture, in prayer, in the liturgical life of the Church. We can touch Christ's Heart and feel him touching ours. Only in this personal relationship with Christ, only in this encounter with the Risen One do we truly become Christians. (General Audience, September 3, 2008)

Lectio Divina

Prayerfully reading the scriptures is essential to our devotion to the Heart of Christ. It is in the word of God, as Pope Benedict pointed out, that "we can touch Christ's Heart and feel him touching ours." This is the reason scripture reading is unlike any other kind of reading. We read not so much for information as for formation, opening ourselves to be formed by Christ's Heart present in the Word. In the tradition of the Church, reading scripture like this has a special name—lectio divina.

> *The phrase "heart of Christ" can refer to Sacred Scripture, which makes known his heart.*
>
> **St. Thomas Aquinas**

Pope Benedict said that praying with scripture "is truly capable of opening up to the faithful the treasures of God's word, but also of bringing about an encounter with Christ the living Word of God" (General Audience, September 3, 2008).

The Pope outlined a five-step process for sacred reading in *The Word of the Lord* (VD, 86–87): reading, meditation, prayer, contemplation, and action. First, he wrote that "[the encounter with Christ] opens with the reading (*lectio*) of a text, which leads to a desire to understand its true content: *what does the biblical text say in itself?*" This basic reading of a scripture passage grounds us in the reality, the meaning in context, of a given passage. Pope Benedict added that "without this, there is always a risk that the text will become a pretext for never moving beyond one's own ideas." Part of listening to the Holy Spirit speaking through the scriptures must include some careful reading so that we do not start ripping passages out of context and conforming them to our notions.

The second step, according to Pope Benedict, is "meditation (*meditatio*), which asks: *what does the biblical text say to us?* Here, each person, individually but also as a member of the community, must let himself or herself be moved and challenged." Having listened to what the scriptures said to the community in which they were written, we now open ourselves up to hearing the word spoken to us in our own communities.

After listening to the Word of God, we respond, giving words to how our hearts have been moved by a particular passage. Pope Benedict calls this "prayer (*oratio*), which asks the question: *what do we say to the Lord in response to his word?* Prayer, as petition, intercession, thanksgiving, and praise, is the primary way by which the word transforms us." The "petition" might take the form of sorrow for our sins, which have been brought to light by the scriptures, or it might lead us to ask for the graces necessary to live in the spirit of what we have just read.

> *The Scriptures need to be read and understood in the same spirit in which they were written.*
>
> **William of Saint Thierry**

Moving to the fourth step, Pope Benedict writes, "Finally, lectio divina concludes with contemplation (*contemplatio*), during which we take up, as a gift from God, his own way of seeing and judging reality, and ask ourselves *what conversion of mind, heart, and life is the Lord asking of us?*" In this step we return to quiet listening. We rest in God's presence and open our minds and hearts to the Holy Spirit, asking for guidance, asking how the Word of God can change us as we strive to take on the mind and Heart of Christ, as we try to see all things with the eyes of Christ. He writes, "Contemplation aims at creating within us a truly wise and discerning vision of reality, as God sees it, and at forming within us 'the mind of Christ' (1 Cor 2:16)."

Finally, to the traditional four-step method of lectio divina, Pope Benedict adds an important fifth step, reminding us that prayer should lead to action. "We do well also to remember that the process of lectio divina is not concluded until it arrives at action (*actio*), which moves the believer to make his or her life a gift for others in charity." If we truly receive the Word of God, we will experience not only a transformation of our minds and hearts, our deepest thoughts and feelings and desires, but also a change in how we live. Receiving the Word in this way, we renew in ourselves the Heart of Christ. Lectio divina results in our being who we were truly baptized to be—the Body of Christ.

The one who did this most perfectly and whom the Second Vatican Council called the "type" and "outstanding model" of the Church is Mary (*LG*, 53). In the conclusion of his reflection on lectio divina, Pope Benedict holds up the Blessed Virgin Mary.

> We find the supreme synthesis and fulfillment of this pro-
> cess in the Mother of God. For every member of the faith-
> ful Mary is the model of docile acceptance of God's word,
> for she "kept all these things, pondering them in her heart"
> (Lk 2:19; 2:51); she discovered the profound bond which
> unites, in God's plan, apparently disparate events, actions
> and things. (*VD*, 88)

As Mary received the Word into her Immaculate Heart and then gave flesh to the Word in her life, so all Christians are called to be open to the Word, to Christ speaking through the scriptures, and to allow the living Word to transform the way they live their lives.

Ignatian Contemplation

St. Ignatius of Loyola in his famous *Spiritual Exercises* also offers a method of going deeper in our prayerful reading of scripture. He invites us to use the gift of the imagination. In a prelude to a week-long meditation on the life of Jesus, Ignatius invites us "to ask for what I desire" ("The Third Prelude" of the Second Week of the *Exercises*). With each meditation we are to seek the following grace: "an interior knowledge of Our Lord who became human for me, that I may love him more intensely and follow him more closely." Or, in the words of the beautiful song "Day by Day" from the musical *Godspell*, we desire "to see thee more clearly, love thee more dearly, follow thee more nearly—day by day."

Ignatian contemplation asks to go beyond the thoughts of our minds to the movements of our hearts. Using the imagination, we pic-ture the scenes in the gospels, going so far as to make "an application of the five senses"—seeing the scene, hearing what is said, becoming aware of its smell, and touching whatever is there to touch. Such imaginative prayer is designed to take us beyond the abstract knowledge of the head to the affective knowledge of the heart.

Whether Jesus Christ appears as a weak, fragile child or as the all-powerful; whether he is being affectionate with the little children or severe with the Pharisees, all is unified and rooted in one single aspect which is that of love; it is there that the person of Christ has a perfect unity and its greatest depth.

Pedro Arrupe, S.J.

Then St. Ignatius invites us to go deeper still by becoming a character in the gospel scene we are contemplating and by interacting with the other figures in the story. By entering into the action, we go from mere observation to encounter.

St. Ignatius ends each meditation with a colloquy or heart-to-heart talk. As he put it, "a colloquy is made, properly speaking, in the way one friend speaks to another, or a servant to one in authority—now begging a favor, now accusing oneself of some misdeed, now telling one's concerns and asking counsel about them" (*Spiritual Exercises* 54). St. Ignatius compares this colloquy to the conversation we might have with close friends, in which we share the desires and concerns of our hearts with them and listen to their hearts as they are expressed in their loving care and counsel.

Encountering the Very Heart of Jesus

Ignatian contemplation will nurture in us an intimate, heart-centered relationship with Christ. But we can go deeper still. We can go far beyond the gospel scene by entering through prayerful imagination into the very Heart of Jesus.

How can we accomplish something so wonderful? First, think for a moment about what moves you. What brings a lump to your throat or a tear to your eye? What touches you so deeply that your body can't help expressing the deep feelings at the core of your being? What situations might lead you to say to another person, "My heart goes out to you"? If you feel sorrow or compassion for others, how much more does Jesus whose heart is divine as well as human? His heart went out to people who were suffering. He felt all that we feel in the face of suffering, but with a pure and divine intensity.

I received some insight into the way we can enter into the Heart of Jesus through an actor named Bruce Marchiano. In his book, *In the Footsteps of Jesus,* Marchiano describes how he had been chosen to play the role of Jesus in a film version of the Gospel of Matthew produced by The Visual Bible, a group that is producing a word-for-word dramatization of the scriptures. Like any good actor, Marchiano knew that he had to enter into the character he was playing. He couldn't approach a scene and think, "Now what would Jesus do here?" He had to become the character that he was playing—Jesus—so that his performance would be convincing. His acting coach had told him that "the journey from the head to the heart is a journey of a thousand miles."

Marchiano was supposed to take that journey from the head to the heart in order to become Jesus in front of the cameras. But he was stymied. He didn't feel that he had really entered into the mind and Heart of Jesus—what Jesus thought and felt—and he felt his acting would suffer from it. So he prayed, "Lord, show me what it all looks like through your eyes." Marchiano describes how his prayer was answered. For a split second, he said, as he looked out at the crowd, he could feel all of Jesus' human emotion with divine intensity. He was given the grace to enter deeply into the Heart of Jesus. He said he believed God protected him by limiting his experience of Jesus' heart to just a split second. Anything more would have been overwhelming. Marchiano wrote,

> It was so awful a thing—I don't have words to describe to you how incredibly awful it was. I remember when it happened, it was as if the wind got knocked out of me; I couldn't breathe, and my heart just broke. It broke on a

level I never knew existed, and I just started shaking and weeping.

What had Marchiano experienced? He wrote,

> What I "saw" in that moment was not with my eyes—it was something in my heart. And the only way I can put it into words is to say it was a sea of people living lives in ways He didn't plan. People living lives away from His love, away from His care; outside of His goodness, His embrace, His plans, purposes, and hopes for them.

Marchiano concluded his description of the experience with these words: "And there can be no doubt what I tasted was just a drop of water in the oceans of the universe compared to what it truly feels like for Him."

By asking for the Holy Spirit to reveal the Heart of Jesus to us through our imaginations, we too can enter more deeply into his interior. We too can feel his feelings and think his thoughts.

The Movements of Jesus' Heart

Now let's look at some of the movements within the Heart of Jesus that we find in the gospels. Time and again we have scenes like the one that Marchiano described. In Matthew we read, "At the sight of the crowds, his heart was moved with pity for them because they were troubled and abandoned, like sheep without a shepherd" (Mt 9:36). Jesus experiences deep sorrow for people who are lost and struggling to find their way, who are burdened by poverty, and who experience rejection by religious authorities. A few chapters later Jesus offers them his peace. "Come to me, all you who labor and are burdened, and I will give you rest. Take my yoke upon you and learn from

> *Jesus, make my heart like unto Yours, or rather transform it into Your own Heart that I may sense the needs of other hearts, especially those who are sad and suffering.*
>
> **St. Faustina Kowalska**

me, for I am meek and humble of heart; and you will find rest for yourselves. For my yoke is easy, and my burden light" (Mt 11:28–30).

Jesus has compassion on the hungry crowds following him. Before miraculously feeding thousands with bread and fish, Jesus tells his disciples, "My heart is moved with pity for the crowd, for they have been with me now for three days and have nothing to eat" (Mt 15:32).

In the presence of death and grief, "Jesus wept" (Jn 11:35). The setting is the raising of Lazarus, a close friend of Jesus and the brother of Martha and Mary of Bethany. Jesus had delayed his response to Martha and Mary's message to him, "Master, the one you love is ill." During the delay, Lazarus had died. Why did Jesus delay? As he told his disciples, "This illness is not to end in death, but is for the glory of God that the Son of God may be glorified through it" (Jn 11:4). Jesus knew he was going to raise Lazarus and in that way reveal his divine power over life and death and that this miracle would give glory to his Father. So why did he cry? The movement of his heart here is deeper than a sentimental sadness. It involves a movement at the depths of his heart in the face of all human suffering and sorrow symbolized in the death of his close friend Lazarus. We see this when John says, "When Jesus saw her [Mary] weeping and the Jews who had

> [Jesus'] heart expresses not only that he is divine love made visible, but also that the deep red blood of human emotion runs in his veins in no way different from the way it runs in ours.
>
> **Raymond Moloney, S.J.**

come with her weeping, he became perturbed and deeply troubled" (Jn 11:33). This reaction is repeated a few verses later where we read, "So Jesus, perturbed again, came to the tomb" (Jn 11:38). According to scholars the Greek word that the New American Bible translates as "perturbed" literally means "he snorted in spirit." Others translate it as "he groaned in the spirit" (King James Version); "he was greatly disturbed in spirit and deeply moved" (New Revised Standard Version); "he was moved with indignation and deeply distressed" (New English Bible); and "Jesus said in great distress, with a sigh that came straight from the heart" (Jerusalem Bible).

Clearly Jesus feels in the depths of his heart all human sorrow and pain. He is compassionate in the original Latin sense of the word—he *suffers with* broken humanity. And he is angry.

The Anger of Jesus

People often think anger is a sin, but it isn't. Anger can lead to sin, but the feeling, the angry movement of one's heart, is not sinful. Consider Jesus at the tomb of Lazarus. Along with deep sorrow, Jesus experiences indignation. He is angry at the plight of humanity burdened by sin and death and under attack by evil forces. The right response to evil and injustice is anger.

We see the anger of Jesus in several other places in the gospels. He is impatient with people who are blind to his identity as God-Made-Flesh, the embodiment of God who is Love. Thus, when his disciples are unable to heal a possessed boy (Mk 9:14–29), he angrily asks, "O faithless generation, how long will I be with you? How long will I endure you?" Then, in response to the boy's father whose request is full of doubt ("if you can do something"), Jesus says, "'If you can!' Everything is possible to one who has faith."

Another time, at the Last Supper, Jesus is impatient with his disciples. Philip says to Jesus, "Master, show us the Father, and that will be enough for us." Jesus responds: "Have I been with you for so long a time and you still do not know me, Philip? Whoever has seen me has seen the Father. How can you say, 'Show us the Father'? Do you not believe that I am in the Father and the Father is in me?" (Jn 14:8–10). Jesus is impatient because he wants so much more for his disciples. He wants them to know him, who he is and his love. But they are blind.

We also see Jesus' anger in the cleansing of the Temple, a scene which appears in all four gospels (Mt 21:12–17; Mk 11:15–19; Lk 19:45–46; Jn 2:13–22). When Jesus comes upon people changing money and selling goods in the Temple, his heart is filled with anger, and he acts on it strongly. He turns over the tables, scattering the coins, and then he makes a whip of cords and drives the animals out of the holy place.

It may look like Jesus has lost his temper in this scene, but his anger is both appropriate and justified. Why? First, God's dwelling place, the Temple, is being desecrated with greedy activity unworthy of God. Second, the moneychangers are exploiting the poor people who came to the Temple to fulfill their religious obligations by paying the Temple tax and offering animal sacrifices. The moneychangers charged them an exorbitant rate to exchange their foreign currency for local currency. Then the people had to pay an inflated price for the animals for sacrifice. In the house of God, of all places, people were being cheated. Understandably, Jesus' heart is moved with indignation. His anger shows his love. When people are being exploited, the opposite of love is not anger but apathy.

The Mercy of Jesus

Although he could be angry over sin and the harm it causes people, Jesus' heart is also full of mercy. Before telling the parable of an unforgiving servant (Mt 18:21–22), Jesus talks with Peter about forgiveness. Peter asks Jesus how often he must forgive someone who has sinned against him. Peter thinks that he is being especially magnanimous when he proposes seven times, but Jesus responds, "I say to you, not seven times but seventy-seven times" (or "seventy times seven" in some translations). The number he uses is symbolic of fullness or infinity. This is Jesus' way of telling Peter *not* to keep score, not to set a limit on forgiving someone who repeatedly hurts him and asks for forgiveness. Jesus ends the lesson by affirming that we all must be as forgiving as God is. If we do not forgive, Jesus says, "so will my heavenly Father do to you, unless each of you forgives his brother from his heart" (Mt 18:35).

Would Jesus ask something of Peter that he was not prepared to do himself? Of course not. In his dying breaths he even forgives those who are killing him, praying, "Father, forgive them, for they know not what they do" (Lk 23:34). The Heart of Jesus is filled with mercy and Jesus challenges his followers to have hearts that are also filled with mercy.

The Joy of Jesus

We've looked at sorrow, impatience, anger, and mercy in the Heart of Jesus. What about pleasure? What about joy? To my way of thinking, a disproportionate amount of religious art depicts Jesus looking sad, stern, and unapproachable in his sorrow. Happily, the revelation of the Sacred Heart of Jesus invites us to see and experience the warmth of Jesus. Although we do not see it illustrated very often, clearly Jesus did a lot of smiling and laughing. Otherwise he would not have had children gathering around him, nor would the crowds have flocked to him.

The actor Bruce Marchiano describes this quality of Jesus. "Yes, Jesus smiled; yes, Jesus laughed. Jesus smiled bigger and laughed heartier than any human being who's ever walked the planet."

Think of all the "sinners and tax collectors" who came to Jesus and hung on his every word. Would they have done so if Jesus wasn't the most engaging personality they'd ever met? Would they have invited Jesus to their parties if he never smiled, if his very presence put a damper on the pleasures of life and human happiness? Just the opposite. When making up their invitation list they made sure that Jesus was on it. You can just imagine them putting the list together and one of them saying, "Yeah, let's invite Jesus! Remember what he did at that wedding feast in Cana?"

Jesus enjoyed life and all its legitimate pleasures. He came to bring life, a fullness of life that begins here on earth with true joy and reaches its climax at the wedding feast of heaven, the eternal banquet.

What did Jesus most enjoy doing? What brought a smile to his face and filled him with joy? For a moment, put yourself in Jesus' place and imagine what he felt when he healed people. Imagine the joy it gave his heart to see the man born blind look upon the world and all its beauties for the first time. It was the beauty of Jesus' own face, the face of God incarnate, that the blind man probably saw first. His face surely lit up with the pleasure of sight. Imagine too how Jesus' face reflected the man's joy as he shared in it completely.

Or imagine the deaf man hearing music and birds singing for the first time, full of the pleasure of sound and the new means of communication that was now possible for him. Or imagine the joy it gave Jesus to heal the leper, the man who had been isolated from humanity and human touch for so long. In healing him, Jesus reached into his isolation and touched him, and by that action Jesus in the eyes of Jewish Law made himself unclean. But he did it to give this man the first human touch he'd experienced in a long time. The healed man, not able to put his feelings into words at that moment, leapt with joy. Imagine how Jesus shared that joy with him.

Yet, though all these healings gave Jesus the greatest pleasure, I think there was something that brought him even greater joy. In Mark's gospel, we read how four men carried their paralyzed friend to Jesus for healing. When they could not enter the crowded doorway, they climbed the roof and lowered their friend down right in front of Jesus as he was teaching. Mark writes, "When Jesus saw their faith, he said to the paralytic, 'Child, your sins are forgiven'" (Mk 2:5). Now put yourself in the place of the paralytic and be honest: Wouldn't you be disappointed with what Jesus just said? There you are hoping to be healed of your paralysis, and all Jesus offers you is forgiveness of your sins. Perhaps you'd say, "That's nice, Jesus, but what I really want is to walk." But in saying what he said, Jesus is showing us his priorities. For him spiritual healing is more important than physical healing. Despite their wonderful healings, someday the eyes of the man who had been blind would close again in death, the ears of the man who had been deaf would be shut, and the skin of the man who had been a leper would turn to dust. Beyond performing mere physical healings, Jesus wanted most of all to touch the immortal part of the human person—the spirit. Spiritual healings had to give Jesus greater pleasure than physical healing.

Jesus told several stories to help us understand the sheer joy that spiritual healing gave him. When Jesus spent time with sinners, hoping to bring them spiritual healing, the Pharisees and scribes grumbled and complained. So Jesus tells them three stories about three lost things—a sheep, a coin, and a son. In each case the finding of what was lost gives the seeker great joy (Lk 15). But the joy of finding something valuable on earth like a sheep or money, Jesus says, pales in comparison to the joy in heaven when a sinner, who was lost, is found. The joy in heaven with "rejoicing among the angels of God" (Lk 15:10) is the joy in Jesus' heart when he can bring spiritual healing to people. It's the joy that Jesus shares with the Father who sent the Son into the world not to condemn people, but to save them (see Jn 3:17).

The Attractiveness of Jesus

What made Jesus so attractive to people that they flocked to be with him? It had to have been more than a free lunch of bread and fish, more even than good wine. Jesus had something that drew people. We want that something. By praying with the scriptures, we can appreciate better what was going on in the Heart of Jesus, what was moving him to say and do what he said and did. We want his thoughts and feelings to fill our imaginations and our hearts. We want our hearts to be like his.

> It is invaluable to converse with Christ and, leaning against Jesus' breast like his beloved disciple, we can feel the infinite love of his Heart.
>
> **Blessed John Paul II**

People were so attracted to Jesus that they wanted to know his secret. His secret of living a full and joyous life was simply that he knew who he was. He was completely at home with himself. He knew himself to be the beloved Son of the Father. He was in touch, at every moment, even the moment of darkness in that Garden called Gethsemane, with the love of the Father for him. Grounded in this identity, he did not have to hide or to posture in any way. He put on no masks. He was a man of integrity. He was at peace with himself. What you saw is what you got.

Our devotion to the Sacred Heart should lead us to that same place. As we live in union with Jesus, we will know ourselves as beloved children of the Father, brothers and sisters and friends of Jesus. So grounded, we will be at peace. One with Jesus, we will think with his mind and feel with his heart. Experiencing the movements of his heart as we prayerfully read the scriptures, we know him better, love him more deeply, and follow him more closely. Entering into his heart, we pray that we may be able to say what St. Paul said in summing up his goal in life, "I live, no longer I, but Christ who lives in me" (Gal 2:20).

Prayer Exercise: Lectio Divina

I offer the following example of prayerful and imaginative scripture reading, lectio divina, to help you incorporate it into your own spiritual practice. Remember, though, that lectio divina is a personal and open-ended exercise. Let the Holy Spirit lead you.

1. As you approach the place where you will read and pray, make the Sign of the Cross and ask the Holy Spirit to guide you.

2. Sit comfortably and be quiet. A speeding car needs room to stop, so take time to slow down and be quiet. Breathe deeply, letting your racing thoughts roll past you. Imagine a sunset over a glassy lake. Or focus on a holy picture or a candle flame.

3. Ask for the grace to see Jesus with the eyes of your heart so you can know his love for you and for all.

4. Slowly read this gospel passage: Mark 1:40–42

> A leper came to him (and kneeling down) begged him and said, "If you wish, you can make me clean." Moved with pity, he stretched out his hand, touched him, and said to

him, "I do will it. Be made clean." The leprosy left him immediately, and he was made clean.

5. Imagine the scene: There is a place outside the village, and the path that Jesus and his disciples are walking. Imagine the man with Hansen's disease (leprosy) approaching them. His whole body is covered with open sores. The apostles and others who are following Jesus are frightened by the disfigured man. They step back. But Jesus does not move. The leper draws closer to Jesus, then kneels. Jesus watches him and waits. The leper speaks. "If you wish, you can make me clean." Now Jesus walks up to the kneeling man, reaches out, and touches him. Jesus says to him, "I do will it. Be made clean." Immediately the leprosy leaves the man. His skin becomes as smooth as a child's. All sores and lesions are gone. He rises from his knees and jumps up with a shout, tears streaming down his cheeks. Now close your eyes and ponder it.

6. Now review the scene from the leper's point of view. Go ahead and put yourself in the place of the leper. How do you feel as you approach Jesus? Are you sad? Are you afraid? Do you feel that this disease, as the ancients often did, is a punishment from God? Yes, you feel all of this. And you are so lonely. Exiled from your community, even your own family, you have had no close contact with people in years. You also feel far from God. You are forbidden to go to the synagogue or the Temple. But for the moment you allow yourself to hope against hope that the man coming down the path can heal you. They say he has healed others. You are desperate to believe, but you fear you will be disappointed. Even if this Jesus is able heal you, will he want to? He is surrounded by people. He is probably too busy for you. What makes you think that you might be one of the blessed ones he heals? But you have to try. Overcoming your fears, you approach, kneel, and speak to Jesus. "If you want, you can make me clean." Jesus looks at you for a long moment. Then he reaches out and touches you on the arm. You see it but you can hardly feel it because the disease has deadened the nerves on your skin. Now Jesus is saying something. He is speaking

to you. He says that he does want to heal you, and then he simply commands you to be clean. At that moment, you feel the touch of Jesus' fingers on your arm. How is it you can suddenly feel that human touch? Are you healed? You are overwhelmed with emotion. You look at your hands. They are clean of all sores. You touch your face with your fingers. Perfectly healed. This is the greatest happiness you have ever known. You are so grateful to Jesus. You spring to your feet and shout for joy.

7. Again review the scene, but this time as you do so enter into the Heart of Jesus. Do it boldly, but prayerfully. Now, as the leper approaches, you, as Jesus, feel no fear, no disgust. You see in this one man all of suffering humanity. All men and women, like this man, are alienated from one another and from God. But you are concentrating on this one man in his particular plight. You see his disease is far advanced. You understand how very painful it has been for him. You know what he has gone through all these years. You know how the fear arose in his heart when he first discovered the symptoms of leprosy and tried to hide it. You know how he left his family to protect them from exposure to this terrible and contagious disease. You know where he has been living, moving from desolate place to desolate place, far from people. Your heart shares in that suffering in a way that only a heart that is both human and divine could. You feel deep pity for the leper. You hear the words, "If you wish, you can make me clean." It breaks your Heart. You want to say to the man, "Do you doubt that I would want to heal you? You know so little about the love of God. Of course I want to heal you!" Now, as Jesus, you reach inside the man's isolation and touch him. Your contact with the disease immediately removes it. The man is physically transformed before your eyes. You feel his happiness. You see his amazement, his smile and his tears. As you shared completely in his suffering, you now share completely in his joy and his gratitude. You too are smiling. You are happy to be doing the work of your Father.

8. Having entered more deeply into this scene from the gospel and into the Heart of Jesus, reflect on what it means for you. Ask yourself, for example: How have you been healed? How do you need healing now? How are you called to share the sorrows and joys of others?

9. Close your prayer with a heart-to-heart talk with Jesus. Share with him your fears, your sorrows, and your joys. Share your gratitude for his compassionate love and the ways it has touched you. Ask that your heart might be more like his, praying, "Jesus, full of compassion and mercy, make my heart like yours. Amen."

5 / The Eucharistic Heart of Jesus

St. Luke tells the story of how the risen Jesus met two disciples who were on their way from Jerusalem to the town of Emmaus. The disciples were depressed—understandably so, because all their hopes had been shattered when Jesus was crucified. As they walked, a man they didn't recognize as Jesus joined them. First he listened to their concerns, and then he showed them scriptural passages describing how the Messiah's suffering would bring vindication and victory. Jesus' teaching moved them deeply. Afterwards they said to each other, "Were not our hearts burning within us while he spoke to us on the way and opened the scriptures to us?" (Lk 24:32).

Similarly, as we've seen, our own reading of the scriptures can lead us into an intense experience with the fiery love of Jesus. Such an encounter begins in the part of the Mass we call the Liturgy of the Word, and it's an encounter with the Heart of Jesus that we can deepen through daily lectio divina.

But there is more. Do you remember how the two disciples on the way to Emmaus recognized Jesus? "And it happened that, while he was with them at table, he took bread, said the blessing, broke it, and gave it to them. With that their eyes were opened and they recognized him" (Lk 24:30–31). This chapter explores the way the Liturgy of the Eucharist opens our eyes to know Jesus intimately, increasing our devotion to his heart.

Jesus in the Eucharist

After we meet Jesus in the Word, we encounter him even more deeply in the second part of the Mass, the Liturgy of the Eucharist. In this part of the Mass we give thanks to the Father, joining ourselves to Jesus' perfect offering. The word *eucharist* means "thanksgiving." In the Eucharist we remember the sacrificial love of Jesus, and we give thanks by offering ourselves—all that we have and all that we are. And having offered all, we receive all—Jesus himself, his Body and Blood, soul and divinity, including his Sacred Heart.

As he named October 2004 to October 2005 the "Year of the Eucharist," Blessed John Paul II described how Jesus in the Eucharist draws us into his Sacred Heart. "The presence of Jesus in the tabernacle must be a kind of *magnetic pole* attracting an ever greater number of souls enamored of him, ready to wait patiently to hear his voice and, as it were, to sense the beating of his heart" (*MND*, 18).

In the Blessed Sacrament we still can meet Jesus today and draw close to his heart, as St. John did at the Last Supper.

The Amazing Gift of His Heart

Devotion to the Sacred Heart of Jesus is preeminently a eucharistic devotion. As we have seen, Jesus is alive and active, speaking to us, in the first part of the Mass, the Liturgy of the Word. But in the second part of Mass, the Liturgy of the Eucharist, Jesus takes us deeper into the mystery of his living Heart. In the Eucharist, the Word becomes flesh once again. Jesus himself becomes present to us and for us. Aflame with love in his heart for us, he gives himself to us, enveloping us once again with love.

What Jesus does in the Eucharist is nothing short of *amazing*, a word that Blessed John Paul II often used in conjunction with the Eucharist. Jesus gives himself completely to us in order to transform us. The more we appreciate this amazing mystery of love, the more we will open to its grace and be transformed by it.

Speaking through the prophet Ezekiel, God made a great promise—twice. In Ezekiel 11:19, he says, "I will give them a new heart and put a new spirit within them; I will remove the stony heart from their bodies, and replace it with a natural heart." Then several chapters later, he repeats his great promise, making it personal. "I will give you a new heart and place a new spirit within you, taking from your bodies your stony hearts and giving you natural hearts" (Ez 36:26). He makes the promise personal in this version by using the words *you* and *your* several times. But to whom is he talking? Was this promise ever fulfilled? When was anyone given this kind of spiritual heart transplant? In Jesus all these questions are answered. The great promise is fulfilled in Jesus who gives us a new heart, his own Heart, in the Eucharist.

Let's spend some time with this amazing thought, reflecting on the eucharistic Heart of Jesus and what happens at every Mass.

The Eucharist and the Sacred Heart

Pope Pius XII, in his encyclical *On Devotion to the Sacred Heart* (*Haurietis Aquas*), explained how devotion to Christ's Heart increases our appreciation of the Eucharist.

> Fervent devotional practice towards the Heart of Jesus will beyond all doubt foster and advance devotion to the Holy Cross in particular, and love for the Most Holy Sacrament of the Altar. We can even assert—as the revelations made by Jesus Christ to St. Gertrude and to St. Margaret Mary clearly show—that no one really ever has a proper understanding of Christ crucified to whom the inner mysteries of His Heart have not been made known. Nor will it be easy to understand the strength of the love which moved Christ to give Himself to us as our spiritual food save by fostering in a special way the devotion to the Eucharistic Heart of Jesus, the purpose of which is—to use the words of Our predecessor of happy memory, Leo XIII—"to call to mind the act of supreme love whereby our Redeemer, pouring forth all the treasures of His Heart in order to remain with us till the end of time, instituted the adorable Sacrament of the Eucharist." For "not the least part of the revelation of that Heart is the Eucharist, which He gave to us out of the great charity of His own Heart." (*HA*, 122)

While devotion to the Heart of Jesus increases devotion to the Eucharist, devotion to the Eucharist also increases devotion to the Heart of Jesus. Pope Paul VI makes the connection beautifully in his apostolic letter *The Unfathomable Riches of Christ* (*Investigabile Divitias Christi*).

> We especially desire, however, that through a more intense participation in the august Sacrament of the altar, a greater devotion be given to the Sacred Heart of Jesus, whose outstanding gift is the Eucharist. For it is in the sacrifice of the Eucharist that our Savior Himself—"always living to make intercession for us" (Heb 7:25)—is immolated and received, whose Heart was opened by the lance of the

soldier and from which was poured out on the human race
a stream of precious blood and water.

More recently, Blessed John Paul II was concerned that the Church
had grown cold toward the Holy Eucharist. That concern prompted
him to write the encyclical *Ecclesia de
Eucharistia* and call for a Year of the
Eucharist. Although he did not live
to see it, that graced year ended with
a Synod of Bishops that gathered to
discuss "The Eucharist: Source and
Summit of the Life and Mission of
the Church." Two years later Pope
Benedict issued his summary of the
Synod's discussions in his apostolic
exhortation *Sacramentum Caritatis*. There Pope Benedict said that
the Eucharist is a mystery to be believed, a mystery to be celebrated,
and a mystery to be lived.

*The ultimate purpose of
Eucharistic transformation
is our own transformation in
communion with Christ.*

Pope Benedict XVI

What exactly do we believe about the Eucharist? How do we celebrate it? And, especially, how do we live this mystery? What comes
to mind first is what we call the Real Presence—that the elements
of bread and wine undergo a substantial transformation during the
eucharistic celebration and actually become the Body and Blood, soul
and divinity of Christ. The Eucharist is not a mere symbol of Christ;
the Eucharist *is* Christ, truly present. The Church has asserted the
truth of the real presence of Christ in the Eucharist throughout the
centuries.

Every Mass is a memorial of the Last Supper. It is something we
do in memory of Jesus, as he asked us to do. In the Eucharist we draw
near, as St. John did at the Last Supper, to the Heart of Jesus. Drawing near to our Lord present in the Eucharist, we draw strength from
his heart just as John did. We find the courage to accept the cross as
it comes to us, courage to live as Christ did.

The Miracle of the Mass

Yet we believe still more. We believe that every Mass is a miraculous re-presentation of the passion, death, and resurrection of Jesus. In his apostolic letter *Stay With Us, Lord* Pope John Paul II put it this way.

> There is no doubt that the most evident dimension of the Eucharist is that it is a *meal*. The Eucharist was born, on the evening of Holy Thursday, in the setting of the Passover meal. . . . Yet it must not be forgotten that the Eucharistic meal also has a profoundly and primarily *sacrificial* meaning. In the Eucharist, Christ makes present to us anew *the sacrifice offered once for all on Golgotha.* (*MND*, 15)

At every Mass a miracle occurs, nothing less. Boundaries of time and space mysteriously disappear. What Jesus did on the cross at Calvary becomes present in the here and now of every celebration of the Eucharist. Thus, we not only draw near to the Heart of Jesus beating in his chest at the Last Supper, we also draw near to his pierced heart on Calvary. In this definitive act of love, Jesus gave his life for our salvation. Even in death, he willed that his heart be opened so that blood and water, signs of the sacramental life of the Church, might gush forth. At Mass we are present as Jesus is lifted up on the cross, suffers, dies, and allows his heart to be opened. At Mass we also encounter the risen Heart of Jesus.

It is truly amazing that God would love the world so much that he would give himself to us in this way. The Eucharist is the sign of love, which Jesus lamented to St. Margaret Mary was ignored and rejected. Love is not loved.

What does Jesus ask of us? When we gather for the Eucharist, mindful of the love of Jesus, we ought to respond by making a gift of ourselves with Jesus to the Father. In this way we can return love for love. By our prayerful participation in the Eucharist, and by living out the transformation that occurs at this celebration in our daily lives, we respond to the appeal of Jesus' heart. We love love in the way he desires to be loved.

It is the nature of love to give everything to the beloved, to hold nothing back. It is the nature of love to be united with the beloved. Jesus, the fullest revelation of the truth that "God is love," did this on the cross and at the Last Supper, and he continues to give all of himself and unite himself to us in the Eucharist.

Responding with the Heart

Jesus' total gift of himself on the cross included his heart. As he hung there, his heart was pierced for all humanity for whom he died. Fr. David Fleming, S.J., wrote that

> intimacy involves the response of my whole person. In true intimacy, everything is shared, nothing is held back. The heart has always represented the response of the whole person. If we say that someone's heart is really not in it, we are saying that he is not giving his all.

The Heart of Jesus was in his passion and death. The Heart of Jesus is in the ongoing re-presentation of that act whenever the Eucharist is celebrated.

Understanding Jesus' whole-hearted offering of himself to us affects how we celebrate the Eucharist and how we live when we leave Mass. The Second Vatican Council called for "active participation" on the part of the congregation at Mass. It is easy to see this only in terms of our external participation—of our liturgical posture, standing, sitting, and kneeling; of our responding to the readings and the prayers of the priest; and of our singing together. Limiting our participation to these externals turns the Eucharist into a boring routine; the liturgy becomes just a rote saying of prayers rather than praying. Active participation requires the engagement of our minds and hearts in prayer. Unless we put our minds and hearts into the celebration of the Mass, we may be physically present at Calvary

For the effect of our sharing in the Body and Blood of Christ is to change us into what we receive.

St. Leo the Great

but, like so many who were there centuries ago, we are oblivious to what is really happening. For the full effects of the sacrament to reach us, we must enter into it.

Our models for this are Mary, the mother of Jesus, and St. John. Both stood under the cross and actively participated in Jesus' life-giving death. Both saw the spear thrust into the side of Jesus and blood and water gush forth for the salvation of the world. Both joined themselves—their sorrows and interior sufferings, their minds and hearts moved by this terrifying act in front of them—and shared in the sufferings of Jesus that saved the world. And both gave witness afterwards to the greatest act of love the world has ever known.

We are called to do the same. We are called to be present, not simply with our bodies, but also with attentive minds and open hearts, to what is re-presented at every Mass in which we participate. Present in this way, we remember what Jesus did for us on Calvary. We remember the saving event that, across the centuries, is brought into the present. We do this, as Jesus himself asked at the Last Supper, "in memory" of him (Lk 22:19 and 1 Cor 11:25).

Eucharistic Transformation

In addition to our belief in what happens at every celebration of the Mass—the re-presentation of Jesus' sacrifice on Calvary and the transformation of the bread and wine into his Body and Blood—we believe something else about the Eucharist. We believe in another transformation—our own.

When he was still Cardinal Ratzinger and serving as prefect of the Congregation for the Doctrine of the Faith, the man who would become Pope Benedict spoke eloquently of the Eucharist's power to effect personal transformation. At a meeting of Italian bishops in 2002, Cardinal Ratzinger spoke about how the transformations that occurred at the Last Supper and at Calvary lead to our own transformation. Referring to Luke's account of the Last Supper (Lk 22:19–20), Cardinal Ratzinger said,

Leslie Benson, twentieth century, USA
Copyright Apostleship of Prayer

Marilyn Hammann, twentieth century, USA
Used by permission.

Daniel Mitsui, 2011, USA
Copyright Apostleship of Prayer.

José María Ibarrarán y Ponce, 1896, Mexico
Copyright David Pappas. Used by permission.

Mosaic from Sacred Heart Manor, Hamden, CT.
Used by permission.

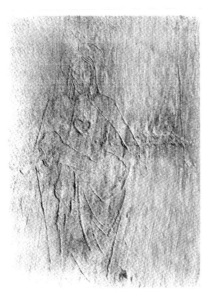

Carving of the Sacred Heart done by Polish Lieutenant Stefan
Jasienski in 1944 at Auschwitz while he was awaiting execution.
Image from *Pozostal ponich slad* by Adam Cyra, Oswiecim, 2006.

Jorge Sánchez, S.J., Mexico
Used by permission.

Br. Mario Venzo, S.J., twentieth century, Italy
Used by permission.

He does not say only: "This is my body," but: "This is
my body, which is given up for you." It can become gift,
because it is given. By means of the act of giving it becomes
"capable of communicating," has transformed itself into
a gift. We may observe the same thing in the words over
the cup. Christ does not say simply: "This is my blood,"
but, "This is my blood, which is shed for you." Because it
is shed, inasmuch as it is shed, it can be given. (Bishops
Conference, Benevento, June 2, 2002)

In those same remarks to the Italian bishops, Cardinal Ratzinger
stated that the act of Jesus' death at the hands of violent men is transformed into a life-giving act that leads to resurrection and eternal life.

[Jesus] transforms, from within, the act of violent men
against him into an act of giving on behalf of these men—
into an act of love. . . . What he teaches in the Sermon
on the Mount, he now does: he does not offer violence
against violence, as he might have done, but puts an end to
violence by transforming it into love. The act of killing, of
death, is changed into an act of love; violence is defeated by
love. This is the fundamental transformation upon which
all the rest is based. It is the true transformation which
the world needs and which alone can redeem the world.
Since Christ in an act of love has transformed and defeated
violence from within, death itself is transformed: love is
stronger than death. It remains forever.

Anticipating the transforming action of his death, Jesus, on the
night before that death, memorialized it forever by transforming
the bread and wine into his Body and Blood. Cardinal Ratzinger
continued,

The gifts of bread and wine, that are the gifts of creation
and at the same time fruit of human labor and the "transformation" of the creation, are transformed so that in them
the Lord himself who gives himself becomes present, in his
gift of self-giving.

Jesus not only gave himself totally for us and our salvation on the cross, but he continues to give himself for us and to us in the Eucharist. That event in time has become an eternal event that transcends time and touches the present whenever people gather to celebrate the Eucharist in memory of Jesus. That memory is not a nostalgic remembering of a great act of love that occurred centuries ago. It's a miraculous representation of that event. In the Eucharist the total gift of Jesus on the cross is made present for us. His Body and Blood are given to us in a way that we can be united to him, through transformed bread and wine. Love desires union with the beloved, and Jesus makes that possible through the Eucharist.

He whom the angels contemplate trembling is he who made himself our food; we are mingled and fused with him, and thus we are made one body and flesh with Christ.

St. John Chrysostom

The transformation of bread and wine into the Body and Blood of Christ leads to the transformation of those who receive him. Cardinal Ratzinger continued,

> The transformation of the gifts, which is only the continuation of the fundamental transformations of the cross and of the resurrection, is not the final point, but in its turn only a beginning. The purpose of the Eucharist is the transformation of those who receive it in authentic communion.

Notice the word *authentic*. Authentic communion with the Lord requires our full participation in the celebration of the Eucharist. Only in this way can the transformation Jesus intended take place. Through the Eucharist, Jesus gives us himself, including his heart, to transform our hearts and in fact the heart of the world. The Eucharist is truly an amazing gift that comes to us from the Heart of Jesus.

Every gift carries with it a responsibility. It can be rejected or ignored. Jesus revealed his Sacred Heart to the saints of old in order to call us to a deeper appreciation of the gift of the Eucharist. He called us to transformation through the Eucharist. The wonderful transforming grace will work its full power only if we allow it, if we give ourselves completely and prayerfully to it. Otherwise, as St. Paul made clear, the results are not simply neutral but negative.

> Therefore whoever eats the bread or drinks the cup of the Lord unworthily will have to answer for the body and blood of the Lord. A person should examine himself, and so eat the bread and drink the cup. For anyone who eats and drinks without discerning the body, eats and drinks judgment on himself. (1 Cor 11:27–28)

You Are What You Eat

In the Eucharist the words of a common adage are realized—"You are what you eat." St. Thomas Aquinas says it better.

> Material food first of all turns itself into the person who eats it, and as a consequence, restores his losses and increases his vital energies. Spiritual food, on the other hand, turns the person who eats it into itself, and thus the proper effect of this sacrament is the conversion of man into Christ, so that he may no longer live for himself, but that Christ may live in him.

Nourished and transformed, we bring the Eucharist into our daily lives. We live now as a new creature with a new heart. Ezekiel's prophecy is fulfilled. We go forth from the Eucharist and live it in thankful praise, offering ourselves, as St. Paul wrote to the Romans, as "a living sacrifice, holy and acceptable to God our spiritual worship" (Rom 12:1). With lives transformed by the eucharistic Heart of Jesus, we love as we have been loved—in a total and self-sacrificing way.

Pope John Paul II stated that this is the standard by which our celebrations of the Eucharist will be judged—by lives that are truly transformed. He wrote,

> We cannot delude ourselves: by our mutual love and, in particular, by our concern for those in need we will be recognized as true followers of Christ (cf. Jn 13:35; Mt

25:31–46). This will be the criterion by which the authenticity of our Eucharistic celebrations is judged. (*MND*, 28)

A Heart for Others

The Eucharist involves an intimate two-in-one flesh union of Christ with each individual who receives him in what we rightly call Holy Communion. Though given to us individually, the Eucharist is not an individualistic gift. It is the gift of Jesus himself, who joins us to his Body and unites us in his heart. He calls us to live not for ourselves but for God and for others. Any devotion to the Eucharist or to the Sacred Heart that results in an individualistic Jesus-and-me piety is a false devotion. The love that Jesus has for each of us is deeply personal and therefore individual. Our devotion to Jesus, our response, will therefore also be deeply personal and unique. But our devotion ultimately leads us to a transformation of any self-centeredness that separates us from others. Transformed by the Heart of Jesus present in the Eucharist, we now have natural, loving hearts and not stony, isolated hearts. Our hearts more and more, as they are transformed by the Eucharist, relate to the world as the Heart of Jesus did—with total self-giving, with a sacrificial love.

> *The liturgy, faithfully celebrated, should be a long-term course in heart-expansion, making us more and more capable of the totality of love that there is in the heart of Christ.*
>
> **Simon Tugwell, O.P.**

In a talk titled "Sunday Eucharist and the Witness of Charity," Pope Benedict speaks of the social dimension of the Eucharist as both obligation and enablement.

> The Eucharist celebrated obliges us, and at the same time enables us, to become in our turn, bread broken for our brothers and sisters, meeting their needs and giving ourselves. For this reason a Eucharistic celebration that does not lead to meeting people where they live, work and suffer,

in order to bring them God's love, does not express the truth it contains. In order to be faithful to the mystery that is celebrated on the altars we must, as the Apostle Paul exhorts us, offer our bodies, ourselves, as a spiritual sacrifice pleasing to God (cf. Rom 12:1) in those circumstances that ask us to make our "I" die and that constitute our daily "altar." The gestures of sharing create communion, renew the fabric of interpersonal relations, impressing them with free giving and with the gift, and permit the construction of a civilization of love. (Address, June 16, 2010)

Burning Furnace of Charity

As the Heart of Jesus present in the Eucharist becomes our own, we are transformed in our entire selves. The union that occurs when we receive Holy Communion sets ablaze in us a "burning furnace of charity," in the words of one of the invocations of the Sacred Heart Litany. Letting St. John Damascene, a great saint of the eastern Church, expand upon the fire imagery, Pope Paul VI stated in his apostolic letter *The Unfathomable Riches of Christ*,

> It is completely fitting that, in the words of St. John Damascene, "we approach it (the Eucharist) with burning desire . . . so that the fire of our desire, having been enkindled from the coals, burn away our sins, and enlighten our hearts, and in the communication of the divine fire we be equally set on fire and deified."

Do we desire to be set on fire in this way? Consider this story told by one of the desert fathers of Egypt.

> Abba Lot went to see Abba Joseph and said to him, "Abba, as far as I can I say my little office, I fast a little, I pray and meditate, I live in peace and as far as I can, I purify my thoughts. What else can I do?" Then the old man stood up and stretched his hands towards heaven. His fingers became like ten lamps of fire and he said to him, "If you will, you can become all flame."

So Jesus said, "I have come to set the earth on fire, and how I wish it were already blazing!" (Lk 12:49).

The Heart of Jesus, on fire with love for the Father and for all humanity, sets our hearts on fire when we are united to him in the Eucharist. The fire in our hearts sets fire to the whole world, to the cosmos. This too is part of the eucharistic transformation.

Transforming the Cosmos

In his 2002 speech to the Italian bishops, Cardinal Ratzinger said,

> By means of us, the transformed, who have become one body, one spirit which gives life, the entire creation must be transformed. The entire creation must become a "new city," a new paradise, the living dwelling-place of God: "God all in all" (1 Cor 15:28)—thus Paul describes the end of creation, which must be conformed to the Eucharist.

God, whose deepest devotion is shown to humanity through the heart of his Son, gives his Son to transform every human being and the entire cosmos. In his apostolic exhortation *The Sacrament of Charity* (*Sacramentum Caritatis*), Pope Benedict said,

> The substantial conversion of bread and wine into his body and blood introduces within creation the principle of a radical change, a sort of "nuclear fission," to use an image familiar to us today, which penetrates to the heart of all being, a change meant to set off a process which transforms reality, a process leading ultimately to the transfiguration of the entire world, to the point where God will be all in all (cf. 1 Cor 15:28). (*SC*, 11)

This may sound like deep mystical theology, and it is. We are drawn by it into the depths of God's loving devotion revealed in the Heart of Jesus. At this depth, we find a love, which St. Paul said, "surpasses knowledge" (Eph 3:19) and yet has practical implications for our daily life. In our next two chapters, we reflect on those implications as we consider the call to continue Jesus' work of reparation. We discover how we can live the eucharistic offering at every moment of our lives.

Prayer Exercise: A Eucharistic Holy Hour

There is no one best way to spend a holy hour. We each relate to God in a unique way. In your holy hour, you give God joy that no one else can give. There is a place in the Heart of Jesus that only you can fill. However you spend an hour (or a minute) in Christ's presence, you will give and receive blessing. You will receive the radiating light and warmth of the Son by simply being in his presence.

There is a story about St. John Vianney wherein he observed an old man come into church and simply sit there for a long time. Curious, St. John asked him what he was doing. The old man replied, "Nothing. I look at him and he looks at me." People in love don't need to say much.

It is good simply to rest in Jesus' presence, like John at the Last Supper, resting his head near the Heart of Jesus. We like to get things done, so we are tempted during a holy hour to feel that we are wasting our time. Yet, five minutes of silent adoration in the Lord's presence communicates more love than sixty minutes of insightful and consoling prayer. The first is a pure act of love on our part, and the latter, while a gift, can become a seeking after spiritual wisdom and pleasures rather than the Lord himself.

The origin of a holy hour spent in Christ's presence goes back to the Garden of Gethsemane when Jesus asked Peter, James, and John to watch and wait and pray while he himself prayed and agonized over his impending Passion. They fell asleep. We want to make up for their neglect of Jesus. In an apparition, Jesus told St. Margaret Mary to rise in the middle of every Thursday night and, in his words, "keep me company in humble prayer to my Father, exactly as I spent that night in agony."

But like the apostles, we may find it difficult to spend an hour in Christ's presence. As our minds race with distractions, we may feel we are wasting our time. The following suggestions for a eucharistic Holy Hour may help.

First, slow down. Just as a racing car requires time and distance to come to a complete stop, so do our racing minds. After you acknowledge Jesus' presence in the Eucharist with a bow, settle into a comfortable position that allows you to rest in his presence, as John did at the Last Supper. Focus on each breath. By slowing your breathing you also quiet your thoughts. With each breath, pray a short invocation—perhaps the Jesus Prayer (breathing in—"Lord Jesus Christ" and breathing out—"Have mercy on me") or the prayer Jesus taught St. Faustina ("Jesus, I trust in you"). When you inhale you might imagine the Holy Spirit, the Breath of God, filling you; when you exhale you might imagine sending the Spirit out upon the people and situations that cause you concern.

> *Transform me into Yourself, O Jesus, that I may be a living sacrifice and pleasing to You. I desire to atone at each moment for poor sinners.*
>
> **St. Faustina Kowalska**

Such resting in his presence may fill your entire time of adoration. As distracting thoughts come up, place them in the Heart of Jesus present in the Blessed Sacrament.

To counter distractions, you may wish to pray using a list of people or situations. Offer each of your concerns to the Lord who said, "Come to me all you who labor and are burdened, and I will give you rest" (Mt 11:28). Or you might use a photo album in which you've placed pictures of loved ones; pictures of Jesus, Mary, and favorite saints; and favorite prayers.

Some people find praying the Rosary helpful. In his apostolic letter *On the Most Holy Rosary* (*Rosarium Virginis Mariae*), Blessed John Paul II called the Rosary "an exquisitely contemplative prayer," and, quoting Pope Paul VI, added that "without contemplation, the Rosary is a body without a soul, and its recitation runs the risk of becoming a mechanical repetition of formulas" (*RVM,* 12). Meditating on the various mysteries of the Rosary, one sees Jesus through Mary's eyes. One "sits at the school of Mary and is led to contemplate the beauty on the face of Christ and to experience the depths of his love." Praying the Rosary in this way in the presence of the Blessed Sacrament can lead us, just as lectio divina does, into the depths of the Heart of Jesus.

You may wish to read scripture or a spiritual book, especially one you read not for information but for the formation of your mind and heart. A book can be a way of listening to the Heart of Jesus speaking to you. It was through reading *The Life of Christ* and biographies of saints that St. Ignatius heard the Lord calling him to follow him more closely. The great contemplative mystic, St. Teresa of Avila, wrote in her autobiography that for eighteen years she experienced great dryness in prayer and as a result "never dared to begin prayer without a book." Reading helped her to focus on God and filled her mind with good and holy thoughts.

6 / Reparation

True devotion to the Sacred Heart of Jesus depends on a proper understanding of *reparation*, an old theological term that is related to atonement, expiation, salvation, and redemption. But don't be afraid. *Reparation* simply means "repair," and that's what Jesus came to do: repair the relationship between God and people. He was "God's Fixer," and he repaired all our brokenness.

Jesus reveals God's love and power in a way we humans can understand it. The Sacred Heart shows us Jesus' essential nature as God's Holy One who loves us so much that he suffered and died in our place to take away the sins of the world. He did so by offering himself to satisfy the just punishment for all sin. His death fixed things up between God and people. And it keeps on fixing even as sin continues. In our devotion to the Sacred Heart of Jesus, we unite ourselves with him and to his sacrifice. We do this in our prayers of offering, as well as in the Mass. When we unite ourselves with Christ, we participate with him in taking away the sins of the world. As we are one with

Jesus, we have the power to make reparation for sins—our own and those of others. With Jesus, we repair the brokenness in our world.

Reparation is so important to our faith and our daily life as Christians that I want to explore it with you at some depth. We shall see that reparation is far more than just a theological concept. Reparation is a way of life that is deeply satisfying. It unlocks for us the joy of following Jesus. It is the essence of our devotion to his Sacred Heart.

The Broken Window

When I was growing up my father used to say, "You get what you pay for." In the years since, I've heard a variation on that piece of advice: "Buy cheap, get cheap." These sayings have to do with the quality of something. We look for good deals, but we worry that what may look like a savings could turn out to be a bad bargain for shoddy goods.

Here's another saying I used to hear growing up. "Somebody's going to pay for this!" It was usually uttered in a moment of anger by someone who felt like a victim of someone else's wrongdoing. Behind this expression is an innate sense of justice. When we are wronged, we feel strongly that something must be done to right the wrong, to bring balance and order into the situation.

For example, my foul ball smashes the neighbor's window. I want to run away, but I tried that in the past and learned that running away just makes things worse. Besides, I know my neighbor is a nice man. So I decide to do the right thing. I knock on his door and confess my guilt. I tell him I didn't mean for the window to get broken. I admit I shouldn't have been playing hardball in the street. I say I'm sorry. As I expected, my kindly neighbor forgives me. But he also reminds me that the window is still broken and needs repairing. It's not enough for me to say, "I'm sorry" and be forgiven. Someone needs to fix that window or pay for it, and that someone should be me. Justice requires it. Until I satisfy justice, my good relationship with my neighbor is broken, or at least strained. Will he ever trust me again if I don't take responsibility for my mistake? It will cost me fifty dollars from my savings to repair the window and the relationship. Fortunately I have fifty dollars in my savings.

But what if I don't have the money, and I have no way to fix the broken window? Because I cannot pay for the damage I caused, the justice that is required in this case must lead to a mercy in which the owner himself suffers. He has to make the repair to the window himself, but even his mercy doesn't really repair our broken relationship. Things are out of balance between us. And I have lost his trust.

Everyday human relationships often require reparation. Sometimes reparation is sought through legal action. As in our social and legal affairs, reparation is also an important element in our spiritual affairs.

Spiritual Laws

People often think that reparation is outdated. They reject it along with an image of an angry, vengeful God. Pope Benedict recognized this in the second volume of his work *Jesus of Nazareth*. Speaking about atonement, or the reconciliation of God and human beings, he writes, "Again and again people say: It must be a cruel God who demands infinite atonement. Is this not a notion unworthy of God?" The Holy Father goes on to affirm that God is not cruel and punishing. God allows us to suffer the consequences of our sinful choices. It is not so much that we are punished for our sins as by them. Our sins carry certain natural consequences that only a miraculous intervention can fix.

The moral laws are as fixed as the laws of physics. For example, I may choose to rebel against the law of gravity, which God has built into his material creation. But when I launch myself off a cliff and flap my arms expecting to soar, I fall to grave injury or even death. It wasn't God who punished me for my rebellion against the law of nature. It was my rebellion against the law of gravity that carried consequences that hurt me.

We see the same dynamic with rebellion against the spiritual laws within us. Just as we have material laws that are built into us by the fact that we are material beings, so do we have spiritual laws that are built into us by the fact that we are spiritual beings. When we rebel against the material and spiritual laws of the universe, we suffer consequences. We pay the price of our foolish decisions.

When I was young I used to think that it was very unfair that I had to suffer the consequences of the sin of Adam and Eve, since their mistake was not my mistake. It didn't seem fair that I was born with original sin. They sinned. Why should I suffer?

My question was based on my delusion of individualism and self-sufficiency. In my childish pride, I had not yet understood that no human being is an isolated individual. The fact is that all humans are interconnected. Why? Because we're made in the image and likeness of God. God is Love, and God's own self is, as we've seen, a communion of three persons. Humanity is created to express or reflect this trinitarian communion. We are created, not to be isolated individuals, but persons in communion. We are created to love one another. On every level we are connected.

> *Contemplating the Heart of Jesus, opened by the soldier's spear as Christ died on the cross for us, we cannot doubt the immense love of God for each and every one of us.*
>
> **Raymond Cardinal Burke**

What one person does affects not only him or herself but others, indeed, all of the human family. What Adam and Eve did had consequences that have rippled down through history, affecting every human who has come after them. Their sin upset the balance and broke trust, and everyone is still suffering from it. We were created to love in the image of God, but we have inherited sin in our nature as well. With each sin that follows that original sin, evil gains momentum.

Something is badly broken and, if it's to be fixed, somebody has to pay. But clearly the damage is beyond our ability to pay for it.

How can the cost of sin be paid? How can the consequences of sin be repaired?

No Cheap Grace

What's clear is that there could be no cheap repair job for humanity's sin. As Pope Benedict wrote in the second volume of his *Jesus of Nazareth*,

> God cannot simply ignore man's disobedience and all the evil of history; he cannot treat it as if it were inconsequential or meaningless. Such "mercy," such "unconditional forgiveness" would be that "cheap grace" to which Dietrich Bonhoeffer rightly objected in the face of the appalling evil encountered in his day.

Bonhoeffer (1906–45) was the German Lutheran pastor who stood with what is known as "The Confessing Church" against the horrors of Nazism. He was hanged by the Gestapo twenty-three days before Germany's surrender in 1945. His book *Discipleship* (1937), later published in English as *The Cost of Discipleship*, addressed the situation that arises when there is forgiveness without justice. He wrote,

> Cheap grace is the grace we bestow on ourselves. Cheap grace is the preaching of forgiveness without requiring a repentance, baptism without church discipline, Communion without confession. . . . Cheap grace is grace without discipleship, grace without the cross, grace without Jesus Christ, living and incarnate.

What does Bonhoeffer mean? He understands that, since God is both Love and Justice, God cannot simply dismiss the first sin and every subsequent sin of humanity. Sin has effects that reverberate through history. Sin needs forgiveness, and its consequences need repair. Balance and order need to be restored. The situation calls for justice. When one child hits another, the hurt child will often strike back. It's only fair. "Even Steven!" But if the hurt child hits back with greater force, the balance of justice will tip the other way and could result in a playground battle. When adults behave this way, we call it a feud, and the injuries compound. The pursuit of justice, without mercy, can quickly descend into vengeance.

Just as individuals, even children, have a sense of justice, we have sometimes pursued justice on a global scale. After great wrongs are committed, we sometimes turn to international courts of law. We saw this when Nazi war criminals were tried at Nuremberg. We have seen it more recently when the perpetrators of genocide in Bosnia or Rwanda were brought to trial before the World Court.

But the greatest wrong of all, the sin of the world—past, present, and future—cannot be brought to justice in a court of law.

True Justice

In his second encyclical, *Saved in Hope* (*Spe Salvi*), Pope Benedict XVI wrote about the problem of repairing the damage of our long history of past wrongs. He quoted the German philosopher and musicologist Theodor W. Adorno (1903–1969) who struggled with the concept of true justice. Adorno, said the pope, "asserted that justice—true justice—would require a world 'where not only present suffering would be wiped out, but also that which is irrevocably past would be undone'" (*SS*, 42).

Of course it is impossible to wipe out all present and past suffering in order to achieve true justice. But what is impossible for humans is possible for God. In the next section of *Spe Salvi*, Pope Benedict continued, "God can create justice in a way that we cannot conceive, yet we can begin to grasp it through faith. Yes, there is a resurrection of the flesh. There is justice. There is an 'undoing' of past suffering, a reparation that sets things aright"(*SS*, 43). What is this reparation that not only does justice but also brings healing? Pope Benedict went on to tell us.

> God is justice and creates justice. This is our consolation and our hope. And in his justice there is also grace. This we know by turning our gaze to the crucified and risen Christ.

> Grace does not cancel out justice. It does not make wrong
> into right. It is not a sponge which wipes everything away,
> so that whatever someone has done on earth ends up being
> of equal value. (*SS*, 44)

We would like, perhaps, to have God just cancel the sin of our ancestral parents, our own sins, and the future sins of the whole world. This would be cheap grace. Forgiveness would be given and received, but the effects of sin would remain. The disorder sin has caused would remain. Something deeper is required—the deep healing we call reparation.

In the second volume of his work *Jesus of Nazareth*, Pope Benedict put it another way. "That which is wrong, the reality of evil, cannot simply be ignored; it cannot just be left to stand. It must be dealt with; it must be overcome. Only this counts as true mercy." Mercy is more than forgiveness. It is also the justice and reparation that bring order back into the disorder and healing to the wounds that sin has caused.

Humanity is incapable of doing this. The task is too great, beyond our ability. Yet, in order for justice to truly be done, humanity had to be the one to right the wrong, to pay the price. There existed an impossible situation. Only God could bring healing, but only humanity could fulfill justice. Thus God did what was beyond all imagining. God became human in order to fulfill all justice and to bring healing to humanity. In Pope Benedict's words,

> The reality of evil and injustice that disfigures the world
> and at the same time distorts the image of God—this real-
> ity exists, through our sin. It cannot simply be ignored; it
> must be addressed. But here it is not a case of a cruel God
> demanding the infinite. It is exactly the opposite: God
> himself becomes the locus of reconciliation, and in the
> person of his Son takes the suffering upon himself. . . . God
> himself "drinks the cup" of every horror to the dregs and
> thereby restores justice through the greatness of his love,
> which, through suffering, transforms the darkness.

Jesus: The Justice of God

This is the great mystery of the Incarnation. The Second Person of the Blessed Trinity became fully human so that as the Word-Made-Flesh, he might save and heal the world. Jesus immersed himself in the destiny of sinful humanity. Fully God and fully human, Jesus alone was able—as he said to John the Baptist who balked at baptizing him—to "allow it for now, for thus it is fitting for us to fulfill all righteousness" (Mt 3:15). He took upon himself the sins of the world, going so far, as St. Paul put it, to become sin. "For our sake he [God] made him [Christ] to be sin who did not know sin, so that we might become the righteousness of God in him" (2 Cor 5:21).

> *In this time of hatred and violence, of injustice and discrimination, the reparation due to the Lord is authentic only if it integrates concern for the poor, promotion of justice, love for the little ones, respect for life.*
>
> **Peter-Hans Kolvenbach, S.J.**

This is the paschal mystery, the incarnation leading to the suffering, death, and resurrection of Jesus. Quoting an early Church hymn, St. Paul described the mystery thus:

> Christ Jesus, who though he was in the form of God, did not regard equality with God something to be grasped. Rather, he emptied himself, taking the form of a slave, coming in human likeness, and found human in appearance, he humbled himself, becoming obedient to death, even death on a cross. (Phil 2:5–8)

Our ancestral parents grasped at "equality with God," for that was the temptation the evil one presented to them. But Jesus, the Son of God, was not interested in grasping his equality with God, though he was and is fully equal to God. Instead Jesus emptied himself of his glory, becoming a human, humbling himself. The disobedience of Adam and Eve, which began the tragically disordered history of sin, was balanced and undone by the obedience of the Son. The obedience of Jesus fulfilled all justice and went beyond it, healing not only that original sin but all the sin that followed it, even our own.

In his Letter to the Romans, Paul compares the reparation Jesus accomplished to the original sin that caused the damage in the first place. After stating that it is "our Lord Jesus Christ, through whom we have now received reconciliation," Paul says,

> But the gift is not like the transgression. For if by that one person's transgression the many died, how much more did the grace of God and the gracious gift of the one person Jesus Christ overflow for the many. And the gift is not like the result of the one person's sinning. For after one sin there was the judgment that brought condemnation; but the gift, after many transgressions, brought acquittal. For if, by the transgression of one person, death came to reign through that one, how much more will those who receive the abundance of grace and of the gift of justification come to reign in life through the one person Jesus Christ. In conclusion, just as through one transgression condemnation came upon all, so through one righteous act acquittal and life came to all. For just as through the disobedience of one person the many were made sinners, so through the obedience of one the many will be made righteous. (Rom 5:11,15–19)

Jesus fulfilled justice in a way that was totally merciful. He did not sponge away evil, but took it into himself and allowed it to be nailed into his own body on the cross, thus transforming it. Jesus saved the world. He made reparation for sin.

Our Role in Reparation

Why is reparation so much a part of Sacred Heart spirituality? After he rose from the dead, Jesus sent his disciples to continue his work of reparation. Two thousand years later, those disciples of Jesus now include us. He sends us to make reparation too. When Jesus appeared to the disciples, he said, "Peace be with you," showed them the wounds in his body by which reparation had been made, and then told them, "As the Father has sent me, so I send you" (Jn 20:21). What did the Father send Jesus to do? To free the world of sin and repair the damage that sin has caused. Jesus sends his disciples to continue this work of reparation.

But, we might ask, if Jesus took upon himself the sins of the world—past, present, and future—what possible role can we play in the work of reparation? Are we supposed to take on the sins of the world too? The answer is found within the mystery of the Church as the Body of Christ. This Body is a reality that Paul describes in his First Letter to the Corinthians. He writes that we "are Christ's body, and individually parts of it" (1 Cor 2:27). Paul goes on to explain that, joined to his body at Baptism, we are connected to one another. Christ is the head of the body and we are the parts. What one part does affects the others. The health of the entire body is affected by the health of its individual members. As members of the Body of Christ, we are now called, if we are true to our deepest identity, to do what Christ, our head, has done. We are to continue his work of loving reparation because, though the world has been redeemed, people continue to sin. People continue to need forgiveness and healing. Jesus' perfect act of obedience is now lived out in our lives. His definitive act of salvation on the cross continues to bring about healing through our own work of reparation. Jesus continues to make reparation for sin, but, one with him, we are called to participate in the work of reparation.

St. Paul again makes this clear in what many find to be a puzzling verse in his Letter to the Colossians. Paul writes, "Now I rejoice in my sufferings for your sake, and in my flesh I am filling up what is lacking in the afflictions of Christ on behalf of his body, which is the church" (Col 1:24). Is Paul saying that Jesus' sufferings and his death on the cross were somehow incomplete or inadequate? What could possibly be lacking in the sufferings of Christ? What Paul is saying is that the only thing lacking in the redemptive sufferings of Christ is our own participation in them. When suffering comes our way, we—members of the body—ought to follow Paul's example and join our sufferings to the head of the body, to Jesus crucified. In this way we mysteriously continue Jesus' work of salvation.

Does this mean we should go out looking for suffering? Not at all. Jesus himself did not seek suffering; he prayed to be spared suffering. There is enough suffering in everyone's life without having to look for more. Like Jesus, we accept our suffering and offer it to God for the good of others.

> *Do not pursue spectacular deeds. What matters is the gift of your self, the degree of love that you put into each one of your actions.*
> **Blessed Teresa of Calcutta**

The bishops of the Second Vatican Council wrote of personal suffering as a science. In their "Message to the Poor, the Sick, and the Suffering" at the end of the final session of the council, they said,

> All of you who feel heavily the weight of the cross, you who are poor and abandoned, you who weep, you who are persecuted for justice, you who are ignored, you the unknown victims of suffering, take courage. You are the preferred children of the kingdom of God, the kingdom of hope, happiness, and life. You are the brothers of the suffering Christ, and with Him, if you wish, you are saving the world. This is the Christian science of suffering, the only one which gives peace. Know that you are not alone, separated, abandoned, or useless. You have been called by Christ and are His living and transparent image.

By sharing or participating in the sufferings of Christ, by uniting our own sufferings to them, we become "his living and transparent image" in the world today. We continue the necessary work of reconciliation and healing.

Consoling the Heart of Jesus

Another aspect of reparation is the tradition of consoling the Heart of Jesus. Can we say that Jesus needs consoling? Can we say that he is suffering even now? Isn't Christ risen and in heavenly glory? How can he suffer and be in need of consolation? How are we to understand this?

Those who love suffer along with those who suffer. As the divine lover of all people, including sinners and unbelievers, Jesus continues to suffer. We are called to console him in his suffering.

We can console Jesus in many ways. Certainly our prayers—expressing our love for him and our desire to repair the damage of sin—are a consolation to Jesus, who is often ignored and forgotten. But prayer is just the beginning of what we can do to console Jesus. The corporal and spiritual works of mercy, by which we care for those who are suffering, are acts by which we console Christ and repair the damage that sin has caused. For what we do unto the least of our brothers and sisters, we also do unto Jesus. In addition, our acts of penance, by which we pray with our bodies as we fast or abstain from particular foods, are also powerful works that repair the ongoing damage of sin, our own and others. Particularly when we offer prayers and acts of reparation for the sins of others, we are following the example of Jesus who offered himself on the cross to take away sin and its effects.

Sometimes people say that God cannot suffer, but lives in unending bliss and the mutual love and glory of Father, Son, and Holy Spirit. And, because God is a great mystery, there is probably a sense in which this is true. But at the same time, the Church recognizes that God does suffer. And, because God suffers, we can console God.

In 1981, before he became pope, Joseph Cardinal Ratzinger stated, "God is a sufferer because God is a lover; the entire theme of the suffering God flows from that of the loving God and always points back to it." He went on, in a footnote, to quote Hans Urs von Balthasar who was quoting Jacques Maritain. "God 'suffers' with us, and in doing so he suffers more than we do; as long as there is suffering in the world, he shares this suffering, he experiences 'com-passion.'"

God is Love, and it is the nature of love to suffer with the beloved when he or she suffers. This is *compassion*, which comes from the Latin meaning "to suffer with." Again, St. Paul's teaching about the Body of Christ can help us understand God's compassion. Describing the connectedness, the solidarity, within the Body of Christ, Paul writes,

> God has placed the parts, each one of them, in the body as he intended. If they were all one part, where would the body be? But as it is, there are many parts, yet one body. . . . God has so constructed the body as to give greater honor to a part that is without it, so that there may be no division in the body, but that the parts may have the same concern for one another. If one part suffers, all the parts suffer with it; if one part is honored, all the parts share its joy. (2 Cor 12:18–20, 24–26)

As head of the body, Christ is connected to the parts. Where one part of the body suffers, Christ the head suffers with it. And, since Christ has a heart that is human and divine, he feels all we feel but with divine intensity.

In a parable about the judgment, Jesus himself asserted the mystery of his own suffering along with others who suffer. Jesus makes it clear that he identifies with any of his "least brothers and sisters" who are suffering and in need (Mt 25:31–46). Whatever is done to help them, he says, is done to help him. Whatever is left undone, leading to further suffering, leads to Jesus' further suffering; for he and his brothers and sisters, parts of his body, are one.

We again see Jesus' solidarity with the suffering in the question he asked Saul on the road to Damascus. "Saul, Saul, why are you persecuting me?" When Saul asked who was asking, Jesus replied, "I am Jesus, whom you are persecuting" (Acts 9:4–5). Jesus didn't ask Saul why he was persecuting his followers or his disciples. He asked Saul why he was persecuting *him*, for he and his body, the Church, are one. He therefore suffers with all his members who are being persecuted.

From these scripture passages we can see that in a mysterious way God suffers with suffering humanity. We can say that the Heart of Jesus is broken by the wounds that are experienced in his body.

But does Jesus suffer with non-Christians, the many who are not baptized, who are not members of his body? Taking as our guide the Second Vatican Council document on *The Church in the Modern*

World, we can answer that "yes," Jesus does suffer with all people, no matter who they are, what they believe, or what they do. Pope John Paul II liked to quote this passage from the document, "By His incarnation the Son of God has united Himself in some fashion with every man" (*GS*, 22). Therefore we can say that wherever humanity suffers, Christ suffers. His heart is wounded by the wounds that humanity inflicts upon itself.

To sum up: since God is both love and justice, and since sin has serious effects, God himself paid the price of our salvation. In the person of Jesus, God repaired the consequences of sin. God took upon himself the reparation that was needed to bring order and balance into the universe. The more we are aware of this, the more grateful we will be, and the more we will want to return love for love.

Joined to the Body of Christ, we care for our suffering members and try, following the example of Christ, to make reparation for sin. This is our joy, the joy of Christ himself, of whom the Letter to the Hebrews says, "For the sake of the joy that lay before him he endured the cross, despising its shame, and has taken his seat at the right of the throne of God" (Heb 12:2). Sharing in his work of reparation, we also share in his joy and glory.

Prayer Exercise: Reparation

In your imagination, look out over the entire world. Call to mind its troubled spots—where people are at war, where people are hungry, where people are suffering in any way. Think of the hatred that drives much killing and terrorism. Think of the greed and indifference that is behind the unjust distribution of the world's resources.

Now bring your attention closer to home—your town or city, your neighborhood. Focus on the fears and sufferings of people in your area.

In this prayer exercise, we recognize our sins of commission and omission, and we repent, asking that we may have new hearts to see others as the Sacred Heart of Jesus sees them. Part of our repentance

is committing ourselves to making reparation, to healing the damage
our sins have caused. We pray:

> God our Father, you created us in your own image and like-
> ness. By becoming human, your Son shared in our human
> nature and has united himself with every human being. He
> suffered and died for all, shedding his precious blood for
> everyone who has ever lived or is alive today or who will
> live in the future. Each human being is precious to you, yet
> we have not treated our brothers and sisters accordingly. In
> our thoughts, words, and deeds; in what we have done and
> in what we have failed to do; we have not honored your
> image in ourselves or in our neighbor. Have mercy on us!
>
> Wherever the humanity of persons is not recognized—
> whether in the womb, after birth, or approaching death:
> Lord have mercy!
>
> Wherever the image of God in the human person is
> disfigured or destroyed: Christ have mercy!
>
> Wherever people are treated as objects rather than sons
> and daughters of God, precious enough to die for: Lord
> have mercy!
>
> Father, your Son and our Savior, Jesus Christ, showed
> us that your love for us is infinite. Jesus obeyed your will
> in his suffering and death on the cross, accomplishing for-
> giveness of sins and repairing all the consequences of sin.
> Following Jesus, I offer myself for the continued healing
> of our broken world. Let my offering unite with Christ's
> in reparation for my own sins and those of others. Let me
> love others with the very Heart of Jesus. And, finally, may
> my offering give joy to Jesus, for his offering has given me
> the joy of everlasting life. Amen.

For Further Reflection

Look at your family and yourself. Where do you see sin causing
problems? Like St. Paul, who, even after meeting Jesus face to face on
the road to Damascus and experiencing a life-changing conversion

still struggled, do you still struggle with sin? Do you identify with his words?

> What I do, I do not understand. For I do not do what I want, but I do what I hate. . . . So now it is no longer I who do it, but sin that dwells in me. . . . The willing is ready at hand, but doing the good is not. For I do not do the good I want, but I do the evil I do not want. . . . Miserable one that I am! Who will deliver me from this mortal body? Thanks be to God through Jesus Christ our Lord. (Rom 7:15–25)

When we honestly examine ourselves, like Paul, we are humbled and confused. There is terrible evil in our world that destroys human lives, and the seeds of that evil lie within us as well. As the Russian novelist Aleksandr Solzhenitsyn wrote, "the line dividing good and evil cuts through the heart of every human being."

Today Jesus said to me, "I desire that you know more profoundly the love that burns in My Heart for souls, and you will understand this when you meditate upon My Passion."

St. Faustina Kowalska

Recall the story of King David's sins (1 Sm 11). The root of David's sin is dehumanizing other people. He sees Bathsheba no longer as a person made in God's image and likeness but as an object to be used for his pleasure. He fantasizes about her, and then, when he sees that his fantasy can become reality, he forces her to give herself to him. When she becomes pregnant, David tries to cover his sin by having her husband, Uriah, return from the war, thinking that on this leave Uriah will certainly go home to sleep with his wife. Uriah doesn't, for to do so would have broken the fast from sexual relations that soldiers followed before going into battle. So David dehumanizes him. Uriah is no longer a person made in God's image and likeness, no longer a good and loyal soldier; he has become a problem. What do you do with problems? You get rid of them as quickly as possible. David orders his general to put Uriah in a situation where he will be killed in battle. For David, Uriah is merely an obstacle to his selfish desires.

We are all also tempted from time to time to see others as less than human, as objects rather than images of the Creator. We ignore their needs or treat them with contempt. People become objects for our will or pleasure, or problems and frustrations, rather than sons and daughters of God our Father, so precious that he sent his Son to bathe them in his precious blood.

7 / Living in Union with the Eucharistic Heart of Jesus

W hat's the point? Why are we wasting our time studying this stupid philosophy which has nothing to do with what's really important? We could be out there spreading the gospel and instead we're stuck here in this seminary wasting our time."

Fr. François-Xavier Gautrelet had heard the grumbling for months. He was getting sick of it, and it got even worse after these Jesuit seminarians had read the letters that other Jesuits who were missionaries in India had sent back to France. The letters told of all the great works the missionaries were accomplishing: how the Word of God was being preached and received and thousands were being baptized just like three centuries earlier when St. Francis Xavier himself had arrived there. Christian communities were being formed and children were being taught to read and write, and the gospel was spreading.

"I can't wait to be a missionary like St. Francis Xavier! That's why I joined the Jesuits, not to study philosophy. I can't wait!"

And so on the feast of his namesake, December 3, 1844, Fr. François-Xavier Gautrelet gathered the seminarians, his spiritual directees, for a pep talk. He told them,

> Look, any good that is accomplished on the missions is a spiritual fruit and it needs to be watered by spiritual means. You have those means at your disposal right now. Don't wait to be an apostle! Be an apostle of prayer! Turn everything into a prayer for the work of the missions, for the spread of the gospel and the salvation of souls. Offer to God every prayer of your day. Every work. Your papers and the headaches you get studying philosophy in Latin and trying to understand it all. Offer to God your frustrations, your impatience, and your sufferings. Offer to God the difficulties you face trying to live in a community with all these other guys and the work you do for them when you help serve meals or clean toilets. Offer it all up to God and the missions will be blessed through your prayers, works, sufferings, and even your joys.

The idea caught on. Beginning each day with a Morning Offering prayer and then trying to remember to renew that offering throughout the day gave meaning and purpose to these young Jesuit seminarians who were filled with enthusiasm and energy for the work of the Church. It channeled all that energy into something positive. It turned the negative into a positive. It helped them to see the connection between the Mass they attended every morning and the rest of their day. It helped them to live a eucharistic life.

The heart that resembles that of Christ more than any other is without doubt the Heart of Mary, his Immaculate Mother, and for this very reason the liturgy holds them together for our veneration.

Pope Benedict XVI

About 160 years later bishops from around the world gathered in Rome for the tri-annual Synod of Bishops. This was the eleventh such gathering since these synods began after the Second Vatican Council, and this time the topic they discussed was "The Eucharist: The Source and Summit of the Life and Mission of the Church." Their meeting brought to a conclusion the Year of the Eucharist which Pope John Paul II had called and which he didn't live to see end.

In the documents, which the bishops received ahead of time to help them prepare for their sharing and discussions, could be found Proposition 43, titled "Eucharistic Spirituality and Sanctification of the World." It stated:

> The Eucharist is at the origin of every form of holiness. To develop a profound Eucharistic spirituality, it is necessary that the Christian people, who give thanks through the Eucharist, be aware of doing so in the name of the whole of creation, aspiring to the sanctification of the world, and working for the same. Christian life finds its own path in the Eucharistic celebration. . . . The daily offering (taught, for example, in the Apostleship of Prayer, practiced by millions of Catholics worldwide) can help each one to become a "Eucharistic figure," following the example of Mary, uniting one's own life to that of Christ, who offers himself for humanity.

True devotion to the Sacred Heart of Jesus is, as we've seen, profoundly eucharistic. Recognizing the gifts that have come to us— our natural and supernatural life, our health and talents, the very Body and Blood and Heart of Jesus, the Son of God—we gratefully make an offering of ourselves with Jesus to the giver of all good gifts, the Father. This is the mystery that we believe and celebrate in every Mass. It is a mystery that, as Pope Benedict reminded us in *The Sacrament of Charity*, is to be lived. The spirituality of the Apostleship of Prayer is a simple and practical way to live the eucharistic life embodied in devotion to the Sacred Heart of Jesus.

Christ will not ask us how many things we have done but how much love we have put into our actions.

Blessed Teresa of Calcutta

The Apostleship of Prayer popularized the Morning Offering. It soon found its way onto bathroom mirrors around the world where people would be reminded to make an offering of their day first thing in the morning. What has come to be known as the Traditional Morning Offering, which has undergone a few changes over the years, captures this eucharistic spirituality, which is the basis of devotion to the Sacred Heart.

Traditional Daily Offering of the Apostleship of Prayer

> O Jesus, through the Immaculate Heart of Mary,
> I offer You my prayers, works, joys, and sufferings
> of this day in union with the Holy Sacrifice of the Mass
> throughout the world. I offer them for all the intentions
> of Your Sacred Heart: the salvation of souls,
> reparation for sin, and the reunion of all Christians.
> I offer them for the intentions of our bishops
> and of all Apostles of Prayer, and in particular
> for those recommended by our Holy Father this month.

O Jesus

The prayer begins with what St. Paul called "the name that is above every name," the name at which "every knee should bend of those in heaven and on earth and under the earth" (Phil 2:9–10). This is the name that an angel told Mary (Lk 1:31; 2:21) and Joseph (Mt 1:21) they were to give the child whom Mary had conceived. It is a first-century adaptation of the Hebrew name *Joshua* which means "God helps" or "God saves." By means of this person and this name God showed his loving devotion to the human race. According to the Acts of the Apostles, St. Peter proclaimed shortly after Pentecost, "There is no salvation through anyone else, nor is there any other name under heaven given to the human race by which we are to be saved" (Acts 4:12).

There are many ways in which we can address our Lord at the beginning of the day. There are many exalted titles for him. But with this one word, "Jesus," we remind ourselves that we are called to a personal relationship with him. We are called to the intimacy of friends who are on a first name basis with each other. Jesus, our Lord and Savior, said to his apostles at the Last Supper and to us, "I have called you friends" (Jn 15:15). True friends share everything they have with one another, and as we are about to make an offering of our day and ourselves, we call our Lord by his first name.

Through the Immaculate Heart of Mary

Immediately after addressing our prayer to Jesus we turn to his mother, Mary. Why? Why bring Mary into the picture? Very simply— no Mary, no Jesus. Without a human mother, Jesus could not have taken flesh and been born. The Son of God could not have become the Son of Man. And so, as Jesus came to us through his mother Mary, we go to him through her.

She is our mother too. Traditionally, the Church has seen in the words Jesus spoke from the cross to his closest disciple John words that are addressed to us as well. "Behold your

Participation in the Holy Sacrifice identifies us with his Heart.

The Catechism of the Catholic Church, 1419

mother" (Jn 19:27). Jesus is such a good friend to us and is truly our brother and so he gives to us his own mother. Mother and Son were united not only physically for the nine months that Jesus was in her womb, but also spiritually in the work of salvation. Their two hearts beat as one in love for humanity, united in the work of salvation. Mary stood under the cross that saved the world and united her sufferings to those of her Son for the salvation of souls. And so it is appropriate that as we make our daily offering, we ask her to join us.

Moreover, we make our offering "through the Immaculate Heart of Mary" because she is an example to us of the great faith with which we want to offer our day. St. Augustine wrote that Mary first conceived in her heart what she would later conceive in her womb—the Word of God. Her heart was whole and undivided. Her desires and affections had one focus—God. She was pure, 100 percent purely devoted to the will of God. Thus she said "yes" to God's plan for her and for the salvation of the world that would come through her. We want, as we begin our prayer and our day, to have a pure and undivided heart that seeks only the will of God in our lives.

I Offer You

St. Paul, writing to the Romans, said, "Offer your bodies as a living sacrifice holy and pleasing to God, your spiritual worship" (Rom 12:1). This is what every Christian is called to do—to make an offering of his or her life. This is what it means to not only believe in and celebrate the Eucharist but to live it. Through Baptism we share in the priesthood of Jesus Christ, and the duty of priests is to offer sacrifice and worship to God. Before the time of Christ, the Jewish priests offered animals that were killed and placed on the altar, then set afire so that the flames and smoke would rise as an offering to God above. Now we Christians, joined to the Body of Christ through Baptism and sharing in the priesthood of Jesus, do not offer animals but ourselves—as Jesus did. The difficulty is that as "living sacrifice[s]" we can walk away from the altar! This is an offering we make at the beginning of the day, but it will need to be renewed throughout the day, especially when we encounter something difficult, something that we want to disappear or from which we want to escape. Through this offering we are returning love, embodied in the gift of ourselves, to Jesus who offered himself completely to us and for us on the cross and continues to offer himself to us in every Mass.

My Prayers

We offer Jesus the prayers of our day. Certainly these will be the prayers of our daily devotional life, but in making this offering we

want to call to mind that there will be many opportunities throughout the day for prayer. It could be as we're driving to work or to the
store. It could be while we are waiting in line somewhere. It could be
when we get angry and want to shout at someone but instead offer a
prayer for his or her well-being. It could be when we are tempted by
lust and we offer a prayer for the person who could easily become an
object for our pleasure but whom we instead prayerfully reverence
as a human person made in the image of God. It may be when we
are in the middle of a boring or frustrating meeting, and we silently
pray the Jesus Prayer ("Lord Jesus Christ, have mercy on me!") as
we breathe in and out. There are many opportunities to bring God's
power and grace into our lives and our world by means of short
prayers throughout the day.

Works

We offer Jesus all the work we will do this day. It may not seem
very important. Just like the work of those Jesuit seminarians who
were studying philosophy, it may feel like a waste of time, like it is not
doing anything to advance the work of salvation or God's kingdom.
The task itself is not important, as long as it is not sinful. What is
important is that every task, no matter how seemingly meaningless
or unimportant, becomes an act of love for God. Blessed Teresa of
Calcutta liked to say that what mattered was not doing great things
for God but rather doing everything, especially little things, as an act
of love for God. We don't want to lose any opportunity to show God
our love, and we can do this by offering up our works as acts of love
for him.

Joys

We offer Jesus all the joys, happy moments, and legitimate pleasures of our day. The traditional Morning Offering did not contain
the word *joy*. It seems that a nun wrote to Pope Pius XII complaining
that without the mention of the word *joy* the prayer was more pagan

than Christian, since joy is the hallmark of a Christian. Pope Pius agreed and added the word *joys* to the prayer. We have been saved and have a sure hope of the resurrection because Jesus died and rose for us. He created us for the perfect joy of heaven. And now in our earthly life we even get little glimmers of that joy. If heaven is a big banquet feast as Jesus described it, then the joys of this life are like little appetizers of heaven. Friends share everything with one another, their joys as well as their sorrows. Thus, we do not keep our joys for ourselves but we share them with Jesus who shares our joy, who enjoys seeing us joy-filled.

And Sufferings

Our sufferings are the most difficult of the four things that we offer to Jesus each day. When suffering comes our way, our usual reaction is both to ask God, Why me? and to ask God to take it away. And yet suffering is an inevitable fact of life. It is bound to come our way and we want, by means of our daily offering, to be ready to make of it an offering to God. And it is a very powerful offering.

When I was growing up this was a regular part of being a Catholic. If we fell on the playground and started crying or were not chosen for the team and were off in the corner moping, Sister Domitille would come over and say three words to us, "Offer it up." The author Emily Stimpson once wrote that this isn't Catholic for "Get over it!"; just the opposite. The idea, again, was that when suffering comes our way we have a choice in what we do with it. We can either slip into self-pity or anger, or we can turn the negative into a positive by joining it to the cross of Jesus Christ and thereby contributing to his ongoing work of saving souls.

In his encyclical about hope, *Saved in Hope,* Pope Benedict gently recommends a return to this practice with these words,

> I would like to add here another brief comment with some relevance for everyday living. There used to be a form of devotion—perhaps less practiced today but quite wide-spread not long ago—that included the idea of "offering up" the minor daily hardships that continually strike at

us like irritating "jabs," thereby giving them a meaning. Of course, there were some exaggerations and perhaps unhealthy applications of this devotion, but we need to ask ourselves whether there may not after all have been something essential and helpful contained within it. What does it mean to offer something up? Those who did so were convinced that they could insert these little annoyances into Christ's great "com-passion" so that they somehow became part of the treasury of compassion so greatly needed by the human race. In this way, even the small inconveniences of daily life could acquire meaning and contribute to the economy of good and of human love. Maybe we should consider whether it might be judicious to revive this practice ourselves. (*SS*, 40)

Of This Day

There is great wisdom in the slogan "one day at a time." We offer ourselves to Jesus one day at a time. We let go of the past; it cannot be changed. And we do not get anxious about the future; we may not live to see it. And so all we ever really have is this day and the present moment. Learning to live one day at a time and in the present can be a source of great peace for us. Focusing on the present will help us to live each day well. On the day after he was arrested and began thirteen years in prison, Vietnamese Cardinal Nguyen Van Thuan wrote,

The world needs the Sacred Heart. The world needs human hearts united to the Sacred Heart.
Catherine de Hueck Doherty

I will live the present moment, filling it to the brim with love. A straight line is made of millions of tiny points united to each other. My life too is made of millions of seconds and minutes united to each other. I will perfectly arrange every single point, and the line will be straight. I will live perfectly every minute and my life will be holy.

Like you, Jesus, who always did what was pleasing to your Father. Every minute I want to tell you: Jesus, I love you.

In Union with the Holy Sacrifice of the Mass throughout the World

We offer our day with its prayers, works, joys, and sufferings in union with Jesus' perfect offering of himself. He made that offering once and for all on Calvary, but it is renewed every day in the Holy Sacrifice of the Mass. We may not be able to be present for the celebration of the Mass on any given day, but we can still participate in the Mass spiritually and live the Eucharist by offering ourselves with Jesus to the Father. Moreover, at any given moment, somewhere in the world, Mass is being celebrated. At any given moment we can unite ourselves spiritually with the renewal of Jesus' offering that is being celebrated somewhere. It is this union that gives significance, eternal significance, to the moments of our day. It is here that we find the meaning and purpose of the most mundane moments of our lives. They may seem small, but just like the five loaves and two fish which Jesus multiplied to feed thousands, so even the little, seemingly unimportant activities of our lives, in the hands of Jesus, will play a part in his great and ongoing work of salvation.

I Offer Them for All the Intentions of Your Sacred Heart

At this point in our prayer we mention specific intentions for which we are offering our day as a prayer. We begin with the intentions that are in the Heart of Jesus. Our reflection on the Word of God—in which we try to enter more deeply into the mind and Heart of Jesus, into his thoughts and feelings as he looks out upon the world—helps us here. As Christians, members of the Body of Christ, we want to have his mind and heart, his thoughts and feelings, his values and attitudes. These are embodied in his heart, the very core of his being. In our prayer and our life we want to unite our heart to Jesus' heart. We want to share his desires and intentions for humanity.

What are some of these intentions? We can pause and consider those things that come to our minds as things that must be very dear to the Heart of Jesus, but the traditional Morning Offering continues by naming some of them.

The Salvation of Souls

This is the reason that God took flesh, was born, lived, died, and rose to new and eternal life. He did this for me, for all humanity. He did this to save us from sin and death. And after his resurrection, he told his disciples that "as the Father has sent me so I send you" (Jn 20:21). What did the Father send his Son to do? To redeem the world from sin and death. To reconcile humanity to God. To save souls. When we say "souls," we ought to keep in mind that human beings are a mysterious composite of a

> *The heart-to-heart with Jesus broadens the human heart on a global scale.*
>
> **Blessed John Paul II**

material or physical body and an immortal soul. Jesus came not only to save our immortal souls but also our bodies. By his resurrection he offers to us the promise that we will one day live body and soul in heaven. We are not meant to be bodiless souls but embodied souls. In our daily offering we offer ourselves for this intention and commit ourselves to living our day in such a way that we will not stray from the path that leads to eternal life. Our prayer for the salvation of souls includes our own. We cannot offer ourselves for the salvation of others and then jeopardize our own salvation. We pray that we and all people may accept the salvation that Jesus won for us through his death and resurrection.

Reparation for Sin

We've already discussed the importance of reparation—that it is a way we join Jesus in his work of reconciliation. Sin hurts people and damages relationships, our relationship with God and with our

neighbor. Sin has effects and consequences. We want to make reparation or to repair the damage that our sins and the sins of others have
done. In the twelve-step program of Alcoholics Anonymous, there
is a step toward recovery that involves making amends to those who
have been hurt by one's bad choices and behavior. Sometimes such
direct amends are not possible because communication with the party
who has been hurt will lead only to more hurt. And in some cases the
people who have been hurt are deceased. The offering in reparation
for our sins can do on a deep spiritual level what cannot be done in a
direct way. Moreover, it's been said that sometimes the best amends is
to live a good life that makes up for the hurt that was caused. Offering ourselves for reparation also means that we commit ourselves to
fighting against our temptations, weaknesses, and sins so that we do
not add to the hurt and suffering that sin causes. And we imitate Jesus
who, though completely sinless and therefore having no damage for
which he was responsible, offered himself to repair the damage of others' sins, in fact, the sins of all. We offer ourselves to repair the damage
that our sins, the sins of others, and all sins have caused.

And the Reunion of All Christians

As we enter more deeply into the intentions of the Heart of Jesus,
we have to imagine that the one thing that breaks his heart the most
is the fact that Christianity is divided. The Body of Christ is torn and
bleeding. We are not one as Jesus prayed we should be. "I pray not
only for them [the disciples], but also for those who will believe in
me through their word, so that they may all be one, as you, Father,
are in me and I in you, that they also may be in us, that the world
may believe that you sent me" (Jn 17:20–21). Our scandalous divi-
sions have hindered the missionary work of proclaiming that "Jesus
is Lord." Unity, Jesus said, would help the world believe. Thus our
disunity makes it difficult, if not impossible, for non-Christians to
believe that Jesus is who he said he is. In fact, the bishops at the Second Vatican Council, in their pastoral constitution *The Church in the
Modern World,* said that atheism

stems from a variety of causes, including a critical reaction against religious beliefs, and in some places against the Christian religion in particular. Hence believers can have more than a little to do with the birth of atheism. To the extent that they neglect their own training in the faith, or teach erroneous doctrine, or are deficient in their religious, moral or social life, they must be said to conceal rather than reveal the authentic face of God and religion. (*GS, 19*)

How it must break the Heart of Jesus to see his followers divided and fighting with each other. We offer ourselves to Jesus for this intention of his heart: that Christians may come together in full and visible unity so that the world may believe that the Father has sent Jesus and in believing accept the salvation that Christ won for us.

I Offer Them for the Intentions of Our Bishops

The final part of our prayer draws our attention to the Church both local and universal. We pray first for the bishops, the successors of the apostles. The prophet Zechariah says that if you can strike the shepherd, the sheep will be scattered (Zec 13:7). One of the tactics of the devil is to attack the leadership in the Church. Knowing that they are targeted and vulnerable, we offer ourselves and our day for the intentions of our bishops, praying that they may be kept safe from harm, grow in holiness, and be guided by the Holy Spirit as they lead the Church.

By the blood of his side and of his Heart our Lord watered the garden of the Church, for with this blood he made the sacraments flow from his Heart.

St. Albert the Great

And of All Apostles of Prayer

In the past this phrase used to read "for all our associates" but that term was confusing. Who are our associates? My family? My coworkers? My friends? We certainly want to pray for them and for their health, both physical and spiritual, and especially for their ultimate well-being—their salvation. But the intent of this part of the prayer was to remember all those people around the world who are also making a similar daily offering. Imagine: all over the world there are millions of people praying for you and you are now remembering them as well. What a tremendous network of prayer! No wonder the Holy Father recognized the great potential for prayer support in the Apostleship and began giving it a monthly prayer intention. This leads us to the final part of the Morning Offering.

And in Particular for Those Recommended by Our Holy Father This Month

When St. Ignatius founded the Society of Jesus, the order to which those French seminarians who began the Apostleship of Prayer belonged, he presented himself and his first companions to the pope. He knew there were many needs all over the world and he felt that the pope, as the shepherd of the entire Church, would have a wide and expansive view of the situation of the Church and the world. He would know where the need was greatest, and St. Ignatius wanted the Jesuits to be sent to meet that need.

It is in this spirit that we end our prayer by expanding our horizon to encompass the needs of the universal Church and the world as seen by the pope. In the first decades after the founding of the Apostleship of Prayer, members received a monthly prayer intention. In time, Blessed Pope Pius IX gave his approval to these intentions and claimed them as his own. Then, in 1928, the missionary office of the Church, the Congregation for the Propagation of the Faith, asked Pope Pius XI to add a second monthly intention for the missions. Since 1929, therefore, millions of people around the world have prayed for the general and mission prayer intentions of the pope.

Do these intentions really come from the pope? How does he select them? In the middle of every year the superior general of the Jesuits, who is the international director of the Apostleship of Prayer, enlists the help of his delegate for the Apostleship who lives at the Jesuit Curia in Rome. The delegate solicits from national directors from around the world the concerns that people in their areas have and for which they would like the Church to pray. The international delegate and a group of advisors sort through the various requests, and eventually send a number of them to the pope. He selects the ones he wants, adapts and changes them to express his desires, and even adds some that he feels should be there. These become the general intentions. The missionary office in the Vatican, now known as the Congregation for the Evangelization of Peoples, sends its suggestions for the mission intentions and a similar process is followed. Then, on December 31, at the celebration of Vespers, the pope gives to the superior general of the Jesuits his monthly prayer intentions for the year that follows the new year about to begin. This allows time for the intentions to be translated and publicized.

Papal Testimony

Recent popes have encouraged the Apostleship of Prayer as a way in which all the baptized can be part of the apostolic prayer of the Church. In a 1948 letter to the general director of the Apostleship of Prayer, Pope Pius XII called the Apostleship "the most perfect form of the Christian life." He echoed those words in 1951, writing that the practices of the Apostleship "contain the sum total of Christian perfection." Why? Because it is a eucharistic way of life. Pope Pius XII explained that those who make and live the daily offering

> are not asked merely to recite certain prayers. Their whole lives must be offered to God as a prayer and a sacrifice for the cause of the apostolate. The daily offering of self is the essence of the Apostleship of Prayer. This is perfected by other acts of piety, especially by devotion to the Sacred Heart of Jesus. The daily life of each member is thus converted into a sacrifice of praise, reparation, and impetration [entreaty]. In this way the forces implanted in Baptism are activated and the Christian offers his life as a sacrifice in and with Christ for the honor of God the Father and for the salvation of souls. (Letter, October 28, 1951)

Pope Pius XII did not see the Apostleship of Prayer as an organization in competition with other associations in the Church. Because the Apostleship of Prayer is by nature eucharistic, he saw it as something to which every Christian could commit him or herself. In an address to a 1956 International Congress of the Apostleship, he expressed his hope that "the Apostleship of Prayer . . . be so united to the other pious Associations that it penetrates them like a breath of fresh air through which supernatural life and apostolic activity are ever renewed and strengthened."

Blessed John Paul II also highlighted the eucharistic nature of the Apostleship. Speaking to an international meeting of national secretaries or directors of the Apostleship in 1985, he said,

> The Apostleship of Prayer—which I have known and appreciated for many years—wants to highlight the apostolic value of prayer in the Church. . . . By instilling the spirituality of the "offering" in union with Christ's oblation in the Mass, the Apostolate of Prayer is right in the line of Conciliar teaching which presents the Eucharistic Sacrifice as the foundation, center and culmination of all Christian life. . . . The Apostleship of Prayer can bring a meaningful and concrete contribution to the diffusion, at all levels, of the great and consoling truth that all Christians can be intimately united to Christ the Redeemer by offering their own life to the Heart of Christ.

We ought to be changed into Jesus and wholly united with him, so that all of his may be ours, and all that is ours may be his, our hearts and his, one heart.

Meister Eckhart

He ended his remarks calling the Apostleship "a precious treasure from the Pope's heart and the Heart of Christ."

The daily offering is at the heart of what can be called "a simple and profound way of life." It is simple because it begins with taking one minute each day to make the actual offering. It is profound because it leads us into the desires of the Heart of Jesus and joins our lives to the offering he made of his. The spirituality of the Apostleship of Prayer and its Morning Offering are a practical way to live the Eucharist in daily life.

But it isn't magic. It is not enough to "say" the prayer every morning. What's necessary is that these words not only be prayed but lived. This simple prayer challenges us to go about our day, with its various activities, including recreation, rest, and sleep, seeking God's will in all things. We don't want to make the offering and then take something back during the day. Throughout the day we try to be conscious that every moment of it has been offered to God for some very important intentions.

A Twelve-Year-Old Member

On October 15, 1885, a twelve-year-old French girl put her signature on an Apostleship of Prayer enrollment form. For years this document was buried in an archive in a Carmelite convent in Lisieux, France, only to come to light again at the turn of the third millennium. There, at the bottom of the certificate, was the signature "Thérèse Martin." We know her today as St. Thérèse of the Child Jesus, the Little Flower. As a result of this discovery, the superior general of the Society of Jesus asked the Congregation for Divine Worship and the Discipline of the Sacraments to name this young woman the second patron saint of the Apostleship of Prayer, after St. Francis Xavier on whose feast the organization was founded. Both these saints, representing the active and contemplative apostles of the world, are co-patrons as well of the missions.

I believe that what helped St. Thérèse develop her simple and profound spirituality, for which she was named a Doctor of the Church by Blessed John Paul II in 1997, was the eucharistic spirituality of offering that we find in the Apostleship of Prayer.

Shortly after turning fourteen, while praying in front of a crucifix, Thérèse felt echo in her heart the words of Jesus from the cross, "I thirst." She wrote in her autobiography *Story of a Soul*, "These words ignited within me an unknown and very living fire. I wanted to give my Beloved to drink and I felt myself consumed with a *thirst for souls*."

In her desire to take away Jesus' thirst for souls, Thérèse targeted people whom she felt were most at risk for losing the salvation Jesus won for them. The first was a man named Henri Pranzini, who had murdered two women and a young girl in the course of a robbery. Apprehended, tried, convicted, and sentenced to death by the guillotine, Pranzini was bitter and unrepentant. He refused to see a priest. Thérèse was obsessed with him and began offering all her prayers and works and little sacrifices for him.

The day of his execution, August 31, 1887, came and went. Thérèse had to find out what had happened. Had he repented? Afterwards she wrote, "In spite of Papa's prohibition that we read no papers, I didn't think I was disobeying when reading the passages pertaining to Pranzini. The day after his execution I found the newspaper *La Croix*. I opened it quickly and what did I see?"

She saw that Pranzini had not gone to confession but at the last moment,

> seized by an inspiration, he turned, took hold of the *crucifix* the priest was holding out to him and *kissed the sacred wounds three times!* Then his soul went to receive the merciful sentence of Him who declares that in heaven there will be more joy over one sinner who does penance than over ninety-nine just who have no need of repentance!

Thérèse called Pranzini her "first child" and was convinced that her prayers and sacrificial offerings had played a role in his last-second conversion.

Imagine for a moment what joy Thérèse brought to the Heart of Jesus through all this. She was his instrument by which his grace was able to reach the hardened heart of Pranzini. From this point on, Thérèse continued to live her life as a total offering to God for the salvation of souls.

The Examen

There is another practice that can help us live a eucharistic life of offering. Though we begin the day mindful of the opportunities that lie ahead to do great things for God by making an offering of every moment, and though we try to be mindful of the offering we have made throughout the day, it's helpful to review that offering at the end of the day.

A traditional practice that is incorporated into the Church's Night Prayer or Compline, is an examination of conscience. In this practice we look back on the day to see how we may have sinned or fallen short. We ask pardon for our sins and make a resolution to leave sin behind the next day.

In recent times, an adaptation, which has been called the Examen of Consciousness or simply the Examen, has been proposed. There are various methods and approaches to doing this. What's important is not so much the method but the actual review of one's day.

Such a review can be done at any time that works best for us, either in the evening or just before going to bed, or even the next morning as we begin the new day. It can be done while driving home from work or taking a walk after supper or in the quiet of one's prayer space or while journaling. Beginning with gratitude for our life and the past day and asking for the light of the Holy Spirit to help us see our day as God sees it, we review the day. It may help to imagine watching a taped video of the day and pausing over significant moments or fast-forwarding through the less important ones. We try to see the day that we offered to God with our Morning Offering. What were the prayers, works, joys, and sufferings that we offered? What were the thoughts, words, and deeds of our day? Where did we make an offering that was pleasing to God and how can we see God using that offering for his purposes? Was there anything in the day that we offered which, in retrospect, was not worthy of God? Was there something that we took back, choosing to do something only with ourselves in mind? Were there any moments when we said to God, "No! Not your will but my will be done! I want to do it my way not yours!"

Looking back on the day in this way, we are grateful for the good that we offered to God and ask that, united to the perfect offering of Jesus, it may be multiplied and play a role in the work of salvation. If we found anything in our review that was not worthy of God, we express our sorrow. When we began the day we didn't want something like this to be part of what we offered to God, but there it is. We are sorry and ask for the grace to do better, never to make such an unworthy offering again.

Reviewing the day, we might also ask what God offered to us. How was God present in the moments of the day, in the activities and people of the day? What was God trying to tell us through them? Was God challenging us in any way through the people and events of our day? Virtues are spiritual muscles and like physical muscles they need to be exercised in order to be alive and healthy. Like the muscles of our bodies, the virtues only grow and develop through exercise. God isn't going to answer our prayer for a particular virtue like patience by zapping us with that virtue. Rather, God will give us opportunities to exercise and grow in that virtue. What virtues was God calling us to exercise today? Did we run from that exercise or embrace it in the knowledge that God was using it to help us become the person we were created to be?

Finally, as we reflect on what God offered to us on any given day, we will see the blessings of the day and be filled with gratitude for them. Remember: as Bishop Diadochus told us, the measure of our love for God depends upon how deeply aware we are of God's love for us. We review our day and spotlight the signs of God's love. This moves us to greater and greater gratitude and the desire to return love for love. We end our day ready to return that love by making an offering the next day and every day.

Pope Benedict and Sacred Heart Devotion

June is the month when the feast of the Sacred Heart is usually celebrated and so the entire month is dedicated to the Sacred Heart.

Pope Benedict talked about this on June 1, 2008, in his Sunday Angelus Address. He said,

> I am pleased to recall that this month is traditionally dedicated to the Heart of Christ, symbol of the Christian faith, particularly dear to the people, to mystics and theologians because it expresses in a simple and authentic way the "good news" of love, it is a compendium of the mystery of the Incarnation and Redemption.

Then, encouraging people to grow in their devotion to the Sacred Heart of Jesus, he said,

> Every person needs a center for his own life, a source of truth and goodness to draw from in the daily events, in the different situations and in the toil of daily life. Every one of us, when he/she pauses in silence, needs to feel not only his/her own heartbeat, but deeper still, the beating of a trustworthy presence, perceptible with faith's senses and yet much more real: the presence of Christ, the heart of the world. Therefore, I invite each one of you to renew in the month of June his/her own devotion to the Heart of Christ, also using the traditional prayer of the daily offering and keeping present the intentions I have proposed for the whole Church. (Audience, June 1, 2008)

Notice how Pope Benedict linked Sacred Heart devotion, the daily offering, and prayer for his intentions. This is the spirituality of the Apostleship of Prayer. This is the best way to respond to the love of Jesus, the love that fills his heart. He offered all, and through the Eucharist and living a eucharistic life of self-offering, we respond in the best possible way to that love. We return love for love, the gift of ourselves in return for the gift of himself that Jesus made on the cross and continues to make in every Eucharist. How pleasing this offering is! And how important a role it plays in the continuing work of the Body of Christ!

By living a eucharistic life in union with the Heart of Jesus, we can hope with confidence to hear the words of Jesus. "Come, you who are blessed by my Father. Inherit the kingdom prepared for you from the foundation of the world" (Mt 25:34).

Imagine for a moment the joy that was in heaven when St. Thérèse crossed its threshold. She had lived a short twenty-four years on earth and the last nine of them were spent in a cloistered Carmelite convent. Her final sufferings were terrible, feeling that she was suffocating as tuberculosis ravaged her lungs. No doubt she offered her sufferings up for particular intentions.

Imagine her soul departing from her suffering body and entering into the next life, crossing the threshold of heaven. A great crowd is there to greet and welcome her. No doubt in the front were her own parents, beatified in 2008. But then, way in the back, as I imagine it, is a man who begins (if this is possible in heaven) to make his way to the front of the crowd. He excuses himself, telling people that he must be the first to welcome her. He gets to the front and tells the startled Louis and Zellie Martin, "Please. Please let me be the first to welcome her." Then, as she crosses the threshold, this man comes up to her and says, "Thérèse. Thérèse, thank you. I wouldn't have made it without you. My name is Henri Pranzini." And with that, she crosses into the total joy of heaven.

We all have the opportunities that St. Thérèse had to make a difference in others' lives through the offering of our own. May we not lose any of those opportunities. One of the heavenly joys we will have is seeing the role that the offerings that made up our eucharistic life played in the lives of others, many of whom we may have never met on this side of eternity. One of our heavenly joys will be seeing the joy that we gave to the Heart of Jesus by the offering we have made.

Prayer Exercise: The Morning Offering

There are dozens of versions of the Morning Offering. In making our own daily offering, we can use any of them or pray in our own words. Some members of the Apostleship of Prayer remember (and prefer) the traditional Morning Offering promoted by the Apostleship of Prayer for many decades. In recent years, the international office of the Apostleship has been recommending a contemporary Morning Offering.

However we pray, the important thing is to consciously make an offering of our day, to try to live that offering as we go through our day, and then review the offering we have made as we come to the close of the day. Here is our contemporary Morning Offering.

> God, our Father, I offer You my day. I offer You my prayers, thoughts, words, actions, joys, and sufferings in union with the Heart of Jesus, who continues to offer Himself in the Eucharist for the salvation of the world. May the Holy Spirit, Who guided Jesus, be my guide and my strength today so that I may witness to your love. With Mary, the mother of our Lord and the Church, I pray for all Apostles of Prayer and for the prayer intentions proposed by the Holy Father this month. Amen.

First, following the example of Jesus, the offering is made to God the Father. We pray like Jesus, who taught us to call God "Abba" or "Father," and we recognize as we say "our" that God is the Father of all people. We are children of one God and brothers and sisters of one another.

We offer everything—all that we think and say and do, one day at a time. If our thoughts can be made a pleasing offering to God, our words and deeds will also please him.

We make our offering to the Father in union with the Heart of Jesus who is present in the Holy Eucharist, renewing his total offering of himself for the salvation of the world. In doing this, we pray that we may be united to the Heart of Jesus, share its movements and feelings, and in this way be inspired to live a eucharistic life.

> The Church seems in a particular way to profess the mercy of God and to venerate it when she directs herself to the Heart of Christ.
>
> **Blessed John Paul II**

Having prayed to the Father in union with Jesus, we now ask that the Holy Spirit guide us during the day. By praying for the Holy Spirit's help, we remind ourselves that our thoughts, words, and deeds will be holy only if they are inspired by the Holy Spirit. The Spirit is the bond of love between the Father and Son, and we are empowered to witness to God's love in our daily lives with the help of the Spirit. Moreover, we will only be able to do God's will perfectly if we are guided by the Spirit who led Mary and Jesus.

Finally we pray for the pope's monthly intentions and for our brothers and sisters around the world who, united to us in spiritual communion, are also making an offering of their lives this day. We do not pray alone. We recognize that we are joined by our Mother—Mary—the Mother of Jesus and also the Mother of the Body of Christ, the Church.

Jesus said that unless we become like children, simple and humble, open to our loving Father's care and guidance and not proud and rebellious, we will not enter the kingdom of heaven. The following Children's Daily Offering can help us be more childlike.

> Heavenly Father,
> I offer you this day,
> all that I do and think and say,
> uniting it with what was done
> by Jesus Christ, your only Son. Amen.

For Further Reflection

Fr. Walter J. Ciszek, a Jesuit priest who slipped into the Soviet Union during World War II to fulfill a dream of ministering there, spent over twenty years in the dreaded Lubyanka prison and in exile before being released and returning to his home in the United States. In his book *He Leadeth Me*, Fr. Ciszek wrote about how faith and the practice of the Morning Offering helped him survive his terrible ordeal. He wrote that in my opinion, the Morning Offering is still one of the best practices of prayer—no matter how old-fashioned some may think it. For in it, at the beginning of each day, we accept from God and offer back to him all the prayers, works, and sufferings of the day, and so serve to remind ourselves once again of his providence and his kingdom. If we could only remember to spend the day in his presence, in doing his will, what a difference it would make in our own lives and the lives of those around us! We cannot pray always, in the sense of those contemplatives who have dedicated their whole lives to prayer and penance. Nor can we go around abstracted all day, thinking only of God and ignoring our duties to those around us, to family and friends and to those for whom we are responsible. But we *can* pray always by making each action and work and suffering of the day a prayer insofar as it has been offered and promised to God.

What is this "providence" that Fr. Ciszek says is so important to call to mind? He explains:

God has a special purpose, a special love, a special providence for all those he has created. . . . It means, for example, that every moment of our life has a purpose, that every action of ours, no matter how dull or routine or trivial it may seem in itself, has a dignity and a worth beyond human understanding. No man's life is insignificant in God's sight, nor are his works insignificant—no matter what the world or his neighbors or family or friends may think of them.

8 / Sacred Heart Devotions

A young novice-sister recently said to me that devotion to the Sacred Heart is "the devotion of devotions." She is absolutely correct because it is not one devotion among many. Rather, devotion to the Heart of Jesus is a response to God's devotion to us. Moreover, as we've seen, Sacred Heart devotion is profoundly eucharistic.

In 2001, the Congregation for Divine Worship and the Discipline of the Sacraments published the *Directory on Popular Piety and the Liturgy: Principles and Guidelines.* In it, the Congregation affirmed both the primacy of the Eucharist and the importance of devotion to the Sacred Heart.

In his decree promulgating the *Directory*, the Prefect of the Congregation, Jorge Cardinal Medina Estévez, wrote,

> In affirming the primacy of the Liturgy, "the summit toward which the activity of the Church is directed . . . and fount from which all her power flows," the Second Vatican Council nevertheless reminds us that "the spiritual

life, however, is not limited solely to participation in the Liturgy." The spiritual life of the faithful is also nourished by "the pious practices of the Christian people" (*SC* 10, 12), especially those commended by the Apostolic See.

> *Being converted to Christ, becoming Christian, meant receiving a heart of flesh, a heart sensitive to the passion and suffering of others.*
>
> **Pope Benedict XVI**

A deeper spiritual life helps people's participation in the Eucharist. This is especially true in regards to devotion to the Sacred Heart, which draws us into a deeper awareness of God's love and into an intimate relationship with the Lord. The *Directory*, in the section on Sacred Heart Devotion (166–173), states that this devotion is to the person of Jesus in his deepest reality.

Understood in the light of the scriptures, the term "Sacred Heart of Jesus" denotes the entire mystery of Christ, the totality of his being, and his person considered in its most intimate essential: Son of God, uncreated wisdom; infinite charity, principal of the salvation and sanctification of mankind. The "Sacred Heart" is Christ, the Word Incarnate, Savior, intrinsically containing, in the Spirit, an infinite divine-human love for the Father and for his brothers. (166)

Devotion to the Sacred Heart is a wonderful historical expression of the Church's piety for Christ, both Spouse and Lord: it calls for a fundamental attitude of conversion and reparation, of love and gratitude, apostolic commitment and dedication to Christ and his saving work. For these reasons, the devotion is recommended and its renewal encouraged by the Holy See and by the bishops. (172)

In calling for the "renewal" of devotion to the Sacred Heart, the *Directory* recognized that artistic representations can be a problem because they "no longer respond to the artistic taste of the people" (173). In particular, the *Directory* mentions "certain over sentimental images which are incapable of giving expression to the devotion's robust theological content or which do not encourage the faithful to approach the mystery of the Sacred Heart of our Savior"(173). Thus the Congregation cautioned that particular unappealing expressions of the devotion should not lead the faithful to reject devotion to the Sacred Heart for, "The Sacred Heart is Christ crucified, his side pierced by the lance, with blood and water flowing from it" (173).

After stating that various expressions or "devotions to the Sacred Heart of Jesus are numerous," the *Directory* lists a number that "have been explicitly approved and frequently recommended by the Apostolic See" (171). It lists personal and family consecrations, the Litany of the Sacred Heart, the Act of Reparation, and the practice of going to Mass on the first Friday of the month.

In this chapter, we look at various practices related to devotion to the Sacred Heart. In doing so we will especially keep in mind their communal dimension. Because this devotion is very personal and intimate, there exists the temptation to see it in a very individualistic way. This is especially a danger at a time in history when "individualism" is a particular problem. The danger can be to see the devotion as an individualistic Jesus-and-me experience that excludes others. However, the call to a deep, personal, and heart-centered relationship with Jesus, while it certainly involves sharing the deepest desires and concerns of our own hearts, does not end there. True devotion to the Sacred Heart of Jesus leads us to share the desires and concerns of that heart. As Jesus told St. Margaret Mary, his heart "is so deeply in love with the human race, it spared no means of proof—wearing itself out until it was utterly spent!" As the Heart of Jesus was open to all people, so devotion to this heart opens our horizons to include all people. We see, as we reflect on particular devotions, how this is true.

Personal Consecration

A few years ago I was speaking to a group of second graders and came to the end of my presentation with ten minutes remaining in our time together. I fell back on my standard approach. I asked the group, "Do you have any questions that you've always wanted to ask?" One little boy raised his hand and asked the burning question that had been on his mind. "What was Jesus' middle name?" After confirming that he thought Jesus' last name was "Christ," I went on to explain that Jesus didn't have a middle name like we do and that "Christ" was not his last name but actually a title. It means "Anointed One." I then went on to explain that at Baptism we all became "anointed ones."

Part of the ceremony of Baptism is anointing with sacred chrism, the perfumed oil that is used to consecrate the walls and altar of a new church at its dedication, the hands of a priest at his ordination, and the heads of those being baptized and confirmed. The anointing sets aside the altar and sacred space of the new church and the hands of the priest for a sacred purpose. That purpose involves the worship of God.

Similarly, at Baptism each of us was consecrated or set aside for a holy purpose—to worship God with our lives. We do this, as we've seen, by making and living a daily offering of ourselves in union with Jesus. The prayer that accompanies the anointing is quite instructive.

> God the Father of our Lord Jesus Christ has freed you from sin, given you a new birth by water and the Holy Spirit, and welcomed you into his holy people. He now anoints you with the chrism of salvation. As Christ was anointed Priest, Prophet, and King, so may you live always as a member of his body, sharing everlasting life.

Each of the baptized, joined to Christ and a member of his body, shares in the priestly, prophetic, and royal mission of Jesus. Each of us is consecrated with the sacred chrism, the holiest of oils, perfumed to remind us, as St. Paul wrote in his Second Letter to the Corinthians, "But thanks be to God, who always leads us in triumph in Christ and manifests through us the odor of the knowledge of him in every place. For we are the aroma of Christ" (2 Cor 2:14–15).

So, having been consecrated at Baptism, why do we have the practice of a further consecration to the Sacred Heart? The practice goes back to St. Margaret Mary and St. Claude de la Colombière, though consecrations have been part of the Church from the beginning. Just as consecrating oneself in the Order of Virgins or pronouncing vows of poverty, chastity, and obedience in a convent, monastery, or religious congregation are a way of further living out one's baptismal consecration, so too is consecration to the Sacred Heart. It is a way of responding to the love that fills that heart. It is a way of committing oneself to the Sacred Heart and declaring, "I want to be devoted to you and to live my life as a response to your love for me. I want my heart to be filled with the thoughts and feelings of your heart. I want our two hearts to beat as one so that as I go through my day, I will live it in such a way that other hearts will be set on fire with the love of your heart that is in me." In consecration, we are basically saying to Jesus, "You've given me everything. You've given me your very self. I give myself back to you."

Pope Leo XIII in his encyclical *On Consecration to the Sacred Heart* (*Annum Sacrum*), the encyclical in which he explained why he was going to consecrate the human race to the Sacred Heart, wrote that because we are God's creatures we belong to God. Naturally the question arises: What's the point of giving back to God through consecration what already belongs to him? Pope Leo's answer?

> In His infinite goodness and love, He in no way objects to our giving and consecrating to Him what is already His, as if it were really our own; nay, far from refusing such an offering, He positively desires it and asks for it: "My son, give Me thy heart." We are, therefore, able to be pleasing to Him by the goodwill and the affection of our soul. For by consecrating ourselves to Him we not only declare our open and free acknowledgement and acceptance of His authority over us, but we also testify that if what we offer as a gift were really our own, we would still offer it with our whole heart. (*AS,* 7)

According to Pope Pius XI, writing in his encyclical *On Reparation to the Sacred Heart,* personal consecration is "undoubtedly the principal devotional practice used in relation to the Sacred Heart" (*MR,* 5).

One can make a formal individual consecration simply by praying one of many consecration prayers that are available. In fact, the

Morning Offering is a way of renewing our consecration every day. And, as the Morning Offering leads us to unite ourselves to the intentions of the Heart of Jesus, so our consecration ultimately takes us out of ourselves in order to share the love that is in the Heart of Jesus for all the people for whom he died. Thus it would be a lie to consecrate oneself to the Heart of Jesus and to harbor any resentment or hatred toward anyone. As St. John said, "If anyone says 'I love God,' but hates his brother, he is a liar; for whoever does not love a brother whom he has seen cannot love God whom he has not seen" (1 Jn 4:20). Consecration to the Sacred Heart means seeing others with the eyes of Jesus. It means seeing others as precious to Jesus because he shed his precious blood for them and renews that consecration of himself for their salvation in every Mass.

Admiral Jeremiah Denton is an example of a form of consecration that may appear to be informal but which is very deep indeed. Shot down over North Vietnam on July 18, 1965, he spent almost eight years in a prison camp, four of them in solitary confinement, before being released on February 17, 1973.

> *The most loving heart of our benign Savior is a burning furnace of most pure love for us; a furnace of purifying love, of illuminating love, of sanctifying love, of transforming love, and of deifying love.*
>
> **St. John Eudes**

Admiral Denton grew up with the prayer, "Sacred Heart of Jesus, I place my trust in Thee." In the midst of his confinement, he heard a voice telling him to pray "Sacred Heart of Jesus, I give my life to you." He remembers this clearly because the words he felt called to pray did not include the formal "Thee" but the more familiar "You." He said: "I prayed that prayer over and over again. The more I prayed it, the more I felt I truly was giving my life to the Lord. Then this peace came over me like a warm blanket, and I no longer felt pain—only peace." Years later, after his release, when fellow soldiers and others, some of whom were on their death beds, asked for advice, he told them to pray this prayer that helped him through his ordeal. He reports that it always brought them peace and comfort.

Communal Consecration

Besides individuals, communities, parishes, dioceses, cities, nations, and the human race have been consecrated to the Sacred Heart. In light of the consecration of the universe or human race which Pope Leo XIII called "the greatest act of my pontificate," we might wonder about this. How can individuals who do not know Jesus or who have rejected him be consecrated to his Sacred Heart? The answer is simple: since Jesus died for all, all people are his and can be consecrated to him.

But what does it mean to consecrate whole groups of people, many of whom would reject outright the very idea? It is a way of praying for the salvation of all. In these consecrations we are asking Jesus, the king of all hearts, to reign over the hearts of all whom we consecrate. We are expressing our love for all who are consecrated, asking Jesus to take them and hold them close to his heart like the Good Shepherd carrying the lost ones. It is a way to respond to the heavenly requests that have been made for centuries: pray for the conversion of sinners. We don't exclude ourselves from this group and we pray that Jesus may hold all of us in his heart and bring us all to accept the salvation he won for us on the cross when his heart was pierced open for all humanity. As Pope Leo XIII wrote in the encyclical *On Consecration to the Sacred Heart* in which he announced his intention to consecrate all of humanity to the Sacred Heart, "not only Catholics, and those who have duly received Christian Baptism, but all men, individually and collectively, have become to Him 'a purchased people' (1 Pt 2:9)" (*AS,* 5). With this in mind, we are called to look upon everyone as precious because Jesus shed his precious blood for their salvation.

Another question arises: If Pope Leo XIII consecrated the entire human race to the Sacred Heart, why have new consecrations of places and people, like Pope Benedict XVI's World Youth Day consecration of the youth of the world to the Sacred Heart? Doesn't the human race include future generations as well? Yes, this consecration, in a sense, covers all; but from time to time it is important to renew and re-focus the consecration. It is as though the grace has been given, but in each new generation there is a need to receive that grace, asking that it deepen within us. Again, Pope Leo XIII answers this question. "In His infinite goodness and love, He in no way objects to our giving and consecrating to Him what is already His, as if it were really our own" (*AS*, 7).

Consecration of the Youth of the World

Specifically regarding the 2011 World Youth Day and the consecration of the youth of the world, what can we learn? The document that was created to help people understand and prepare for the consecration is helpful. As we've indicated, there is a hunger in every human heart. It is a hunger for happiness and for love that only God can satisfy. The preparatory catechesis states that

> this search of man's heart ends when one discovers God's Heart. . . . Man's heart "needs" a heart at his same level, a heart that can enter into his history, and, on the other hand, an "all-powerful" heart that can take him out of his limitations and sins. We can say that in Jesus Christ, God has met mankind and has loved us with a "human heart."

In the consecration that took place on August 20, 2011, at the eucharistic vigil, the young people who had gathered, representing the youth of the world, made a declaration "to fix our eyes on Jesus Christ, so that he helps us to live 'planted and built up in Jesus Christ, firm in faith' (Col 2:7)." Like John beneath the cross of Jesus, they declared their intention to contemplate "the open Heart of Jesus on the Cross," experience his love, and become his witnesses.

Clearly, this particular consecration shows us that it is an act of love, an act by which the youth, in solidarity with young people around the world, returned to Jesus love for love. In doing this they committed themselves to living the rest of their lives, as best they can, as living witnesses of the love of God revealed in the pierced Heart of Christ. Anticipating the consecration they wrote, "In this consecration we will touch Jesus, and we will renew the grace of our baptism in which we were immersed in this Love. . . . We will look with his same merciful eyes, so that we are always close to the poorest and the sick, becoming a tangible sign of God's love."

Sacred Heart Badges

It's common for people to carry photos of their family and friends in their wallets or purses. It's a way of saying, "I love them very much, and though we may be physically separated from one another, this photo is a reminder of our love which keeps us close to one another in a deeper, spiritual way." Similarly, one way that people have expressed their devotion or consecration to the Sacred Heart is to carry a badge with an image of the Sacred Heart. This tradition goes back, again, to St. Margaret Mary.

In a letter dated November 3, 1689, St. Margaret Mary wrote to her Jesuit spiritual director, Fr. Jean Croiset. She wrote about how Jesus first appeared to her and revealed his heart which was wounded, encircled by thorns, and surmounted by a cross. She wrote that Jesus told her to make an image of the heart she had seen, and, in her words, "to carry it on my person, over my heart, that he might imprint his love there, fill my heart with all the gifts with which his own is filled." She shared this practice with the younger sisters, and the practice spread.

Since then people have carried small badges of the Sacred Heart of Jesus in their wallets or pockets, have attached them to chains to be worn around their necks, or have pinned them to their garments. The practice has been especially popular in times of crisis, during outbreaks of disease or war. Besides the image of the Heart, there are often the words of two brief invocations. "Sacred Heart of Jesus, thy kingdom come," and "Cease, the Heart of Jesus is with me."

Carrying a holy picture like this should be an act of devoted love and not superstition. There are no guarantees that the person carrying such a badge will avoid dying in a car wreck or catching a disease. The guarantee is much deeper. Using a holy object like this as a sign of love will not go unheeded by the Lord who promised to bless those who are so devoted to him. Having loved him on earth in this way, the assurance is that this love will reach its fulfillment in the kingdom that Jesus said he has prepared for those beloved of him from all eternity.

The Twelve Promises

Throughout her letters to various people, St. Margaret Mary shared special promises that Jesus had made to her regarding those who shared the love of his heart. For example, in a letter of 1689 to her spiritual director, she wrote that her "divine Master" had told her that consecrated religious who were devoted to his heart "won't need to look any further for ways of reviving their first fervor." Priests "who labor for the salvation of souls will acquire the art of touching the hardest hearts, and see their work crowned with success, if they have a tender devotion to the Sacred Heart." And

> lay people, too, will find in this devotion all the help they need: peace in their families, rest amid their toils, the blessing of heaven on all their ventures, comfort in time of trouble. There, in the Sacred Heart, they will find a home and shelter all their life long—but, above all, at the hour of death. A lifetime of tender and true devotion to the Sacred Heart of our Savior and our Judge ensures the blessing of a happy death!

How are we to understand promises like these? Again, as with the badge, they are a call to devotion, not superstition. If people are truly aware of the love of God revealed in the pierced Heart of Jesus, then they will return love for love. They will love God and neighbor as Jesus commanded. This will give them confidence and peace as they go about their daily lives. They will be able to share the riches of the love, which their devotion engenders and in this way touch hard hearts and guide lost souls.

These promises that Jesus made to St. Margaret Mary and which appear scattered throughout her letters have been distilled into what have come to be known as the Twelve Promises. It seems they first appeared in this form in France in 1863 on the cover page of a prayer booklet. The following list of promises was compiled in 1882 by Dayton, Ohio, businessman Philip Kemper. He extracted them from her writings and had his printing company make cards with the Twelve Promises. They became so popular that by 1895 they had been translated into 238 different languages.

1. I will give them all the graces necessary in their state of life.
2. I will establish peace in their homes.
3. I will comfort them in their afflictions.
4. I will be their secure refuge during life, and above all in death.
5. I will bestow abundant blessings upon all their undertakings.
6. Sinners shall find in my Heart the source and the infinite ocean of mercy.
7. Tepid souls shall become fervent.
8. Fervent souls shall quickly mount to high perfection.
9. I will bless every place in which an image of my Heart shall be exposed and honored.
10. I will give to priests the gift of touching the most hardened hearts.
11. Those who shall promote this devotion shall have their names written in my Heart, never to be effaced.
12. I promise thee in the excessive mercy of my Heart that my all-powerful love will grant to all those who communicate on the first Friday in nine consecutive months the grace of final penitence; they shall not die in my disgrace nor without receiving their Sacraments. My Divine Heart shall be their safe refuge in this last moment.

It helps to think of these promises in light of the gospel. Citing several gospel passages (Mt 17:20 and 21:21–22, about faith and prayer in Jesus' name; Mk 16:17–18, about the signs that will accompany the apostles' preaching; and Jn 14:12–14, about doing greater works than the ones Jesus did and asking in his name), the Jesuit theologian Karl Rahner wrote, "Taken in their entirety, these promises affirm and offer no more than our Lord himself promised in the gospel to absolute faith." In other words, the promises that Jesus made to St. Margaret Mary add nothing to those he made when he walked this earth and called people to have faith in his love and to follow him faithfully.

> *The devotion cannot be forced, but seeks to penetrate gently and sweetly by the holy unction of charity.*
>
> **St. Margaret Mary**

Of particular concern is the twelfth promise, called the Great Promise. According to the *Directory on Popular Piety and the Liturgy*, this promise should be seen in the context in which it was made. "At a time when sacramental communion was very rare among the faithful, the first Friday devotion contributed significantly to a renewed use of the Sacraments of Penance and of the Holy Eucharist" (*Directory*, 171). The *Directory* goes on to caution that today "constant instruction" is required so that this practice doesn't become a matter of "mere credulity" or superstition, that it arise from "an active faith," that it not become a substitute for participation at Sunday Mass, and that those who practice this devotion "may undertake their commitment to the Gospel correctly in their lives."

In other words, making the nine first Fridays is not a ticket to heaven. It is not an automatic guarantee. To make the nine first Fridays early in life with the idea of then living an immoral life is not really to practice devotion to the Heart of Jesus. It is to engage in the practice in bad faith. Regarding the promise that people devoted to the Heart of Jesus will not die "without receiving the sacraments," Jesuit Father F. J. Power writes, "This does not mean necessarily the actual reception of the sacrament of the Anointing of the Sick—only the reception of the Sacrament if it is needed 'for a happy death.'"

Like praying in the name of Jesus and expecting to receive whatever is requested, so with the promises: the key is good faith. Through sincere devotion to the Heart of Jesus, the promises will be realized in one's life. They are not magic but the natural consequence of a life lived in union with the Heart of Jesus.

A practical way of promoting devotion to the Heart of Jesus in parishes can be encouraging people to participate in the celebration of Mass on the first Friday of the month. Perhaps a special Mass or Mass time that would allow for greater participation can be scheduled and could be followed by a meal with a brief talk that highlights the love of God revealed in the Sacred Heart of Jesus.

Enthronement or Family Consecration

One of the Twelve Promises to those devoted to the Heart of Jesus involves "peace in their families." Another has to do with blessings coming upon those places where an image of the Sacred Heart is "exposed and venerated." We can find these in seminal form in St. Margaret Mary's letters. In a letter to her mother superior, dated August 24, 1685, she wrote,

> No one who has a deep devotion to the Sacred Heart will ever lose his soul. Since all blessings come from our Lord, they will be lavished especially on those places where an image of the Sacred Heart is displayed to win him love and honor. In this way, he will mend broken homes, help and safeguard families in time of need.

Though family devotion to the Sacred Heart is mentioned in the letters of St. Margaret Mary, it became a common practice among Catholic families two centuries later as a result of one man, Fr. Mateo Crawley-Boevey. Fr. Mateo was born in Peru in 1875, the son of an English father and Peruvian mother. He joined the Congregation of the Sacred Hearts of Jesus and Mary, was ordained in 1898, and was sent to Valparaiso, Chile, where he founded a Catholic university in 1905. He was especially interested in creating a law school where Catholics could be formed to advance the social mission of the Church. One year later, it was destroyed by an earthquake. As Fr.

Mateo dealt with this setback and worked tirelessly to help those who had lost homes, businesses, and loved ones, his health broke. He was sent to Europe to recover.

On June 5, 1907, Fr. Mateo met with Pope Pius X and shared with him a dream that had begun to take shape in his heart. He had been thinking about promoting the social reign of Christ in families. Since society as a whole goes as the family goes, if the reign of the Sacred Heart of Jesus is to be realized in the world, it must begin in families. He wanted to dedicate his life to this goal and would do so if his health returned. Did the Holy Father approve of his plan? The pope responded, "No, no, my son. I do not permit you. I command you, do you understand? I order you to give your life for this work of salvation. It is a wonderful work. Consecrate your entire life to it."

Most sweet Jesus, set on fire my love for You and transform me into Yourself.

St. Faustina Kowalska

With this directive, Fr. Mateo went on pilgrimage to Paray-le-Monial, France. On August 24, 1907, at the age of thirty-two, in the chapel where the revelations of the Sacred Heart to St. Margaret Mary occurred, Fr. Mateo prayed and promised that he would dedicate the rest of his life to this, whether it be short—as it seemed it would be given his illness—or long. As he rose from prayer, he felt cured and began the mission that would consume his attention and energies until his death at the age of eighty-five in 1960.

After the death of Pope Pius X, Fr. Mateo once again sought papal confirmation for his mission. In a letter dated April 27, 1915, Pope Benedict XV wrote to him.

> We have read your letter with interest and likewise the documents that accompanied it. From them we have learned of the diligence and zeal with which for many years you have devoted yourself to the work of consecrating families to the Most Sacred Heart of Jesus, in such a way that while His image is installed in the principal place in the home as on a throne, our Divine Savior Jesus Christ is seen to reign

at each Catholic hearth. . . . Nothing, as a matter of fact, is more suitable to the needs of the present day than your enterprise. . . . You do well, then, dear son, while taking up the cause of human society, to arouse and propagate above all things a Christian spirit in the home by setting up in each family the reign of the love of Jesus Christ. And in doing this you are but obeying our Divine Lord Himself, who promised to shower His blessings upon the homes wherein an image of His Heart should be exposed and devoutly honored.

It is assuredly, therefore, a holy and salutary work to secure for our beloved Redeemer such worship and honor. But that is not everything. It is of the utmost importance to know Christ, to know His doctrine, His life, His Passion, His glory. For to follow Him does not consist in allowing ourselves to be swayed by a superficial religious sentiment that easily moves weak and tender hearts to tears, but leave vices intact. To follow Christ is to be permeated with a lively and constant faith, which not only acts upon the mind and heart, but likewise governs and directs our conduct. . . . Continue therefore, beloved son, in your efforts to enkindle in Catholic homes the flames of love for the most Sacred Heart of Jesus: but likewise and before all else, and this is our wish, endeavor to make this love result from a knowledge of Christ the Lord, and from a greater and deeper understanding of the truths and laws which He Himself has given us.

With these words, Pope Benedict XV made it clear that true devotion to the Heart of Jesus should be life changing and society changing. It involves a deeper awareness of the love of God revealed in Jesus and a response to that love which leads to a virtuous life. John Adams, the second president of the United States, once wrote,

We have no government armed with power capable of contending with human passions unbridled by morality and religion. Avarice, ambition, revenge, or gallantry, would break the strongest cords of our Constitution as a whale goes through a net. Our Constitution was made only for a moral and religious people. It is wholly inadequate to the government of any other.

The goal of devotion to the Sacred Heart and family consecration is to create virtuous people who can transform society and the world.

When Pope John Paul II visited Paray-le-Monial on October 5, 1986, he affirmed the importance of family consecration in building "the civilization of love." He said,

> Yes, thanks to the sacrament of marriage, in the Covenant with divine wisdom, in the Covenant with the infinite love of the Heart of Christ, you families are given the means to develop in each of your members the riches of the human person and of his call to the love of God and men. Welcome the presence of the Heart of Christ, entrusting your home to him. . . . Before the open Heart of Jesus, we seek to draw from him the true love that our families need. The family unit has a fundamental role in the construction of the civilization of love. (Address, October 5, 1986)

The *Directory on Popular Piety and the Liturgy* also makes clear the intrinsic connections between the Sacred Heart of Jesus, marriage, and family life. It describes family consecration as follows: "in which the family, by virtue of the sacrament of Holy Matrimony already participating in the mystery of the unity and love of Christ for the Church, is dedicated to Christ so that he might reign in the hearts of all its members." Notice, this consecration, like others, is a way of deepening the reality of a prior consecration. In this case, the prior consecration is the sacrament of Matrimony by which spouses are consecrated or set apart as witnesses to the world of the intimate love that Christ has for the Church.

Family consecration is often called Enthronement because it involves choosing a prominent place in the home where an image of the Sacred Heart is placed. This is usually done in the course of a prayer service or ceremony. Just as a marriage is more than the wedding, so too with family consecration. It is not a magical act that will lead to the protection and peace of a family. It is a commitment on the part of the family, which gives Christ the King a place of honor in the family, recognizing his authority, and claiming this part of creation for the reign of his kingdom.

It is a good idea for a family considering such a consecration to discuss this, making sure that everyone understands the meaning of this consecration. The family can work together in choosing an image and the place where the image will be "enthroned." It is a good idea, as well, to prepare for the ceremony by going as a family to the sacraments of Reconciliation and the Eucharist. Afterward from time to time, the consecration should be renewed on significant dates—the wedding anniversary and that of the consecration, the Feasts of the Sacred Heart and Christ the King, as part of birthday celebrations, or monthly on the first Friday.

Family consecration can also play a significant role in the prayer life and daily activities of a family. Members can gather together at the beginning of the day and renew the consecration with the Morning Offering prayer. As they leave the house and later return, members can pause in front of the image and pray a short invocation. "All for you, Sacred Heart of Jesus"; "Jesus, I trust in you"; "I am yours and yours I want to be"; "Heart of Jesus, make my heart like yours." As families make decisions about their life together, they should bring their consecration into the picture, asking questions like: "Is this television program or movie worthy of Jesus? With Jesus as the head and heart of this house, how does this activity serve him?" And when conflicts arise between family members, family members should go in front of the image of the Sacred Heart, pray to Jesus, asking for guidance and help to resolve the difficulty, and then continue the discussion mindful of his presence as the Lord of the family. Finally, an evening family meal can be the setting for a daily examen in which members share with one another the prayers, works, joys, or sufferings that were part of the day that they offered to Jesus when it began.

Without love, a house is just a building and not a home. As we've seen, the source of true love is the Heart of Jesus. With Jesus as the center and heart of the family, families will be rooted and grounded in true love and be a source of renewal for society itself, since, as Pope

John Paul II repeated on numerous occasions, the family is the basic cell of society. As a body needs healthy cells, not cancerous cells which do not cooperate with the body but multiply and impose their will on a physical body, so too does society and the Church need healthy families united to the Heart of Christ.

Divine Mercy

Periodically I'm asked, "Is Divine Mercy a new form of Sacred Heart Devotion?" People wonder if they should exchange their Sacred Heart prayer practices for the Chaplet of Divine Mercy and if it's okay to use the image of Divine Mercy when they consecrate their families and homes. At times it can even seem as though the Sacred Heart and Divine Mercy are in competition with one another. How are we to understand the relationship between devotion to the Sacred Heart and devotion to Divine Mercy?

First of all, recall how Jesus has appeared to people throughout the centuries beginning with Saul. In the 1200s he appeared to Bl. Juliana at a time when belief in the Eucharist had begun to wane, and he asked for a new feast in honor of his Body and Blood. Then in the 1600s he appeared to St. Margaret Mary at a time when devotion to his presence in the Blessed Sacrament had grown cold. He revealed his heart on fire with love and asked for a feast of reparation. In the 1930s, during the most merciless century in human history, he appeared to the Polish nun St. Faustina Kowalska and revealed his heart filled with mercy. Just as the revelations of the Sacred Heart to St. Margaret Mary did not replace devotion to the Eucharist which Jesus had called for centuries earlier, and indeed were a further development of that eucharistic devotion, so too with Divine Mercy. It is not a replacement for Sacred Heart devotion but a further development in the expression of God's love.

A cursory reading of St. Faustina's *Diary: Divine Mercy in My Soul* shows the deep devotion that she had to the Sacred Heart of Jesus. The Divine Mercy image that Jesus asked to be painted shows red and white rays emanating from his heart, reminding us of the blood and water that flowed when it was pierced on the cross. According to Robert A. Stackpole, director of the John Paul II Institute of Divine Mercy in Stockbridge, Massachusetts, the Divine Mercy and the Sacred Heart are "so closely bound up with each other as to be *absolutely inseparable*." The reason is simple, as Dr. Stackpole writes, *"Jesus has only one Heart!* His Sacred Heart is His Merciful Heart— they are one and the same."

Thus we can say that devotion to Jesus under the sign of Divine Mercy and devotion to Jesus under the sign of the Sacred Heart are inseparable but not identical. Each has its own feast day—the Friday after Corpus Christi if celebrated on a Sunday for the Sacred Heart and the Second Sunday of Easter for Divine Mercy—and each has a different emphasis and different practices. Though, as we've seen, devotion to the Heart of Jesus has been from the beginning more than a matter of reparation, yet that has become a primary emphasis of this devotion. St. Faustina's *Diary* has elements of reparation. Jesus complains to her in words similar to ones that St. Margaret Mary heard. "Oh, how indifferent are souls to so much goodness, to so many proofs of love! My Heart drinks only of the ingratitude and forgetfulness of souls living in the world. They have time for everything, but they have no time to come to Me for graces." And we hear, "I wait for souls, and they are indifferent toward Me. I love them tenderly and sincerely and they distrust me. I want to lavish My graces on them, and they do not want to accept them. They treat Me as a dead object, whereas My Heart is full of love and mercy." Christ even shows St. Faustina how she could use her sufferings "to offer reparation to God for the souls murdered in the wombs." Love always seeks to make up for what the Beloved is missing and to repair the insults and injuries done to the Beloved, so it is natural that St. Faustina's *Diary* would include elements of reparation. But God's mercy is the primary focus.

Both of these devotions originate in one devotion—God's devotion to humanity. Both come from and lead us back to a deep, heart-to-heart relationship with our Savior. In both we are called to have hearts like the Heart of Jesus—hearts that are merciful in thought, word, and deed. Dr. Stackpole summarizes his belief in the unity of Divine Mercy and the Sacred Heart. "In short, the differences between these two devotions are best described as differences of *emphasis*, for both spring from a common source: devotion to the same Heart of Jesus, overflowing with merciful love for us."

Is it appropriate to use the Divine Mercy image for family consecration? I believe so, as does Dr. Stackpole who writes, "the enthronement of the image of the Divine Mercy is also an enthronement of the Sacred Heart, but that Heart seen under a different aspect."

Thus, in living out one's consecration to the Sacred Heart, either individually or as a family, it's very appropriate to use Divine Mercy prayers. The words that Jesus asked St. Faustina to have painted on the original image—"Jesus, I trust in you"—are a way that we can express our consecration, surrendering to the merciful love of the Sacred Heart. The Three O'Clock Prayer reminds us of the hour when Jesus died and his heart was pierced and is another form of trusting surrender. "O Blood and Water which gushed forth from the Heart of Jesus as a fountain of mercy for us, I trust in you." Lastly, the Chaplet's invocation of God's mercy upon the whole world is interspersed with the prayer. "Eternal Father, I offer You the Body and Blood, Soul and Divinity of Your dearly beloved Son, Our Lord Jesus Christ, in atonement for our sins and those of the whole world." This prayer is eucharistic in nature and when it is prayed, we can unite ourselves to the offering that we are making of "the Body and Blood, Soul and Divinity" of Jesus. In doing this we are making reparation or atonement with Jesus who offered himself in reparation for sin so that God's mercy might flow into the world and heal the damage that sin had caused.

Devotion to the Immaculate Heart of Mary

We've already seen, as we discussed the traditional Morning Offering prayer, that Mary plays an important part in our devotion to the Heart of Jesus. It was in her womb that his physical heart developed.

As Jesus came to us through Mary, so it makes sense to approach Jesus through Mary. Not that we cannot approach him alone, but as he lived perfectly the will of the Father, thus honoring his parents, so do we follow his example and honor his parents. We do so out of our desire to be like Jesus and to have a heart like Mary's.

Blessed John Paul II, during one of his Angelus Messages (September 3, 1989) at a time when he reflected on the different invocations in the Sacred Heart Litany, said, "The heart of Mary is like the Heart of her Son in all things." Pope Benedict XVI echoed these words in his Angelus Message of June 5, 2005. "The heart that resembles that of Christ more than any other is without a doubt the Heart of Mary, his Immaculate Mother, and for this very reason the liturgy holds them up together for our veneration."

This unity of the two hearts of Jesus and Mary is clear in the juxtaposition of their feasts, the Sacred Heart of Jesus on Friday and, the next day, the Immaculate Heart of Mary. This reminds us of their unity, both hearts totally dedicated to the will of the Father, which is the salvation of the world. Devotion to the Immaculate Heart of Mary in one way or another leads us to deeper devotion to the Sacred Heart. As the gospel scene at Cana (Jn 2:5) shows, Mary always tells us, "Do whatever he tells you." Her perfectly obedient heart is united to the obedient heart of her Son and she calls us to be obedient as well.

For this reason some people, as they make their family consecration, do so to the two hearts and have images of both the Sacred Heart and the Immaculate Heart.

Summary

We have looked at some of the primary ways that people have lived out their devotion to the Sacred Heart of Jesus. The key to any devotion is to see it as a response to God's love. It is a concrete and practical way that we respond to God's devotion to us. God is faithful in his devotion and through these various practices we express our desire to be faithful in our response, in our devotion to him. If we engage in these practices in good faith, that is, with a desire to return love for love rather than to have our will be done, then they will lead us naturally beyond ourselves. While they express the unique and deep personal love that Jesus has for each individual, an intimate relationship with him always leads us to share the desires and concerns of his heart. Our devotion leads us to express our devotion not only in moments of personal prayer but throughout our life. We express our love for God by our love for those whom God loves—our brothers and sisters in the human family for whom the Heart of Jesus was pierced.

> *Without love the world is very dark. Let us arise and resurrect the world by bringing love to it and it to God.*
>
> **Catherine de Hueck Doherty**

Prayer Exercise: Family Consecration Prayer Service

The following scripture service from the Apostleship of Prayer can be used by families to consecrate themselves to the Sacred Heart of Jesus, acknowledging him as the head and heart of the family.

Leader: In the name of the Father and of the Son and of the Holy Spirit.

All: Amen.

Reader: The Lord spoke to us through the prophet Ezekiel, saying, "I will give you a new heart and place a new spirit within you, taking from your bodies your stony hearts and giving you natural hearts" (Ez 36:26).

Leader: Lord, as we draw near to you, we remember our sins. We are sorry for all the times we have offended you or ignored your love. Lord, have mercy on us.

All: Christ, have mercy on us.

Leader: Lord, have mercy on us.

All:	Take away our stony hearts, Lord, and give us new hearts, clean and responsive to you.
Reader:	At the Last Supper Jesus said, "This is my commandment: love one another as I love you" (Jn 15:12).
Leader:	Father, make our hearts like Jesus' heart—full of love.
All:	Give us love for one another—and also for our neighbors.
Reader:	As Jesus hung on the cross, his heart was pierced. John wrote, "One soldier thrust his lance into his side, and immediately blood and water flowed out" (Jn 19:34).
Leader:	At that moment, the Church was born. Jesus, you asked all people to be born again by the blood of your sacrifice and the water of Baptism.
All:	Remind us, Lord, that as we are born again of water and blood, we are all members of God's family, the Church.
Reader:	Jesus stood up and exclaimed, "Let anyone who thirsts come to me and drink. Whoever believes in me, as scripture says, 'Rivers of living water will flow from within him'" (Jn 7:37–38).
Leader:	Fulfill this promise in us, Jesus. Fill us with the living waters of your Holy Spirit.
All:	Let us share your Spirit with one another and with everyone we meet.
Reader:	They said to each other, "Were not our hearts burning within us while he spoke to us on the way and opened the scriptures to us?" (Lk 24:32).
Leader:	Jesus, you are the incarnate Word of God. You reveal the Father to the whole world.

All: Give us love for your Word, Lord. Give us light to understand it in our hearts.

If married people are not present, skip this bracketed section.

[Reader: St. Paul exhorted husbands and wives to love each other, "even as Christ loved the Church and handed himself over for her" (Eph 5:25).

Leader: Lord, strengthen the bond of marriage of those here who are married. Always faithful to one another and open to life, let them be one as you are one with your Church.

All: Keep them joyful in their love, Lord.]

Reader: St. Luke describes how the child Jesus lived with his parents in Nazareth where he "was obedient to them . . . and Jesus advanced in wisdom and age and favor before God and man" (Lk 2:51–52).

Leader: Jesus, you asked the children to come to you. Call each of our children to close friendship with you.

All: We are all children, Lord. Help us to honor our parents and obey them in love.

Reader: Jesus said, "Come to me, all who labor and are burdened, and I will give you rest. Take my yoke upon you and learn from me, for I am meek and humble of heart, and you will find rest for yourselves. For my yoke is easy and my burden is light" (Mt 11: 28–30).

Leader: We ask you to give special grace to those who are fragile, elderly, disabled, or sick.

All: Help us remember that we all have needs. Let our needs lead us to rely on you for everything. Let us also support and care for one another.

Reader:	St. Paul wrote, "I urge you therefore, . . . by the mercies of God, to offer your bodies as a living sacrifice, holy and pleasing to God, your spiritual worship" (Rom 12:1).
Leader:	Jesus, you give yourself to us as a living sacrifice every time we receive you in the Eucharist.
All:	In grateful response, we give ourselves to you again this moment. Let us do so each time we receive Communion. Remind us to continue to offer you each day, even each hour, so that your perfect will may be done in each of our lives.
Reader:	St. Paul prayed, "That Christ may dwell in your hearts through faith, that you, rooted and grounded in love, may . . . know the love of Christ that surpasses knowledge, so that you may be filled with all the fullness of God" (Eph 3:17–19).
Leader:	We offer you our whole family, including those who are not able to be here today.
All:	Lord Jesus Christ, come live in the hearts of every member of our family. Increase our love and understanding of your Sacred Heart.
Leader:	Let us honor the Sacred Heart of Jesus. He suffered for us because he loved us. Let him be King of our home.
All:	Jesus, King of our hearts, we worship you.

At this point in the service, an image of the Sacred Heart is brought to a place of honor where the family may kneel, sing a hymn, or join hands together and pray the "Our Father."

Leader:	I thank God for each one of you. I thank God for this family. Let us go in peace, resting now and always in the love of the Sacred Heart of Jesus.

All: Glory be to the Father and to the Son and to the Holy Spirit. As it was in the beginning, is now, and ever shall be, world without end. Amen.

9 / Loving with the Sacred Heart of Jesus

I n May 1965, a song by Burt Bacharach and Hal David made it to
number seven on the hit parade:

> What the world needs now is love, sweet love.
> It's the only thing that there's just too little of.
> What the world needs now is love, sweet love,
> No not just for some but for everyone.

"What the World Needs Now Is Love" captures the universal desire
of every human heart: to be loved and to love.

At World Youth Day in 2011, Pope Benedict XVI consecrated the
youth of the world to the Sacred Heart. The catechetical document
designed to help young people prepare for this consecration acknowl-
edged the desire for love.

> When we enter into the depths of our heart, we always
> find a deep desire: we long for happiness. But we wonder

where and how we can find this happiness. Our experience tells us that this thirst is quenched when our longing for infinity is satisfied. Pope Benedict tells us in his message [for the 2011 World Youth Day]: "Men and women were created for something great, for infinity." This longing for infinity is man's desire of being loved by an endless love.

> *In fact, in the Heart of Jesus God shows that he wants to be understood in his absolute desire to love, forgive, and save.*
>
> **Blessed John Paul II**

What the world needs now is love. We know that, but our experience of love tells us that we are limited and weak and unfaithful. We love one another with finite, not infinite, love. No human love can ultimately satisfy our longings for infinite "endless love." We change, relationships change, and we die, leaving behind loved ones. How can we find infinite love on this side of eternity?

The Answer to Human Longing

God became human in order to bring us this infinite love in a way in which we could receive it. The catechetical document goes on.

> This search of man's heart ends when one discovers God's Heart. On this topic, St. Augustine says: "You made us for yourself, Oh God, and our heart is restless until it rests in you." The concern to which St. Augustine refers is the difficulty we all have in attaining true Love as a consequence of our condition of creatures; we are finite; moreover, we are sinners. Over and over again we run into the difficulty of our selfishness, the chaos of our passions, that throws away this true Love. Man's heart "needs" a heart at his same level, a heart that can enter into his history, and, on the other hand, an "all-powerful" heart that can take him out of his limitations and sins. We can say that in Jesus Christ, God has met mankind and has loved us with a "human heart."

Only a heart that is infinite, that is capable of endless love, could satisfy the deep longing in every human heart. Only a heart that is human can be approached without fear of being overwhelmed and annihilated. We find this heart in Jesus, the Son of God. We find the answer to our longing in the Sacred Heart.

Pope Benedict spoke of God's strategy for sharing his endless love with us.

> In fact, from the infinite horizon of his love, God wished to enter into the limits of human history and the human condition. He took on a body and a heart. Thus, we can contemplate and encounter the infinite in the finite, the invisible and ineffable Mystery in the human Heart of Jesus, the Nazarene. (Angelus Message, June 1, 2008)

Jesus is the answer to the longing of every human heart. The love of his heart is the only love capable of filling our human longing—because it is human, yet infinite, and because it is also divine. Not only does each individual need and desire this love, but the world, taken as a whole, needs it.

Our world is filled with hatred and violence, with apathy and indifference to the plight of so many millions who are suffering the effects of self-centeredness and greed. What it needs, as the song goes, is love. Not just a "sweet" love, but a powerful and transforming love. It needs the love of the sacred and eucharistic Heart of Jesus. Only in this way will hearts of stone become loving hearts. As the preparatory catechesis for World Youth Day 2011 states,

> The biggest expression of how much and in which way God loves us, is the open heart of Jesus on the Cross, as a consequence of the wound on His side with a spear. As the Pope states in his message: "it is from Jesus' heart, pierced on the Cross, that this divine life streamed forth" (WYD message). Thus, in the Cross, Jesus changes our "heart of stone" wounded by sin, into a "heart of flesh" like his: he gives us his Love and, at the same time, he enables us to love with his same love.

"You Shall Draw Waters"

On May 15, 1956, the centennial of the establishment of the Feast of the Sacred Heart for the universal Church, Pope Pius XII wrote an encyclical entitled *On Devotion to the Sacred Heart*. The Latin title of the encyclical is *Haurietis Aquas*, "You shall draw waters." This is a quotation from the prophet Isaiah. "You shall draw waters with joy out of the Savior's fountain" (Is 12:3). That prophecy was fulfilled in the Heart of Jesus from which the abundance of God's love and eternal life flow.

To mark the fiftieth anniversary of this great Sacred Heart encyclical, Pope Benedict XVI wrote of the lasting value of the Sacred Heart devotion. In a letter to the superior general of the Jesuit Order, Fr. Peter-Hans Kolvenbach, he wrote, "After fifty years, it is still a fitting task for Christians to continue to deepen their relationship with the Heart of Jesus, in such a way as to revive their faith in the saving love of God and to welcome him ever better into their lives." Devotion to the Heart of Jesus, Pope Benedict continued, "cannot be considered a transitory form of worship." This is not one devotion among others. It is *the* devotion of all devotions. It is the awareness of God's love that inspires all prayer practices and devotional exercises.

The "mystery of God's love for us," Pope Benedict wrote, constitutes "the content of the worship of and devotion to the Heart of Jesus." It is, in the pope's eyes, "the content of all true spirituality and Christian devotion. It is consequently important to stress that the basis of the devotion is as old as Christianity itself."

This has been our focus in these pages. Devotion to the Sacred Heart of Jesus is really the devotion of the Heart of Jesus to which we respond in proportion to our awareness of that loving devotion of his. The Heart of Jesus continues to go out to us as it went out to the people of his time. His heart was pierced and remains open for all time.

Made in the image and likeness of God who is love itself, we are made for love. But we cannot give what we do not have. We cannot love as we've been loved unless we accept the love of God poured out through the pierced Heart of Jesus. It is, as we've seen, in the Eucharist that we are empowered to love as we remember the passion, death, and resurrection of Jesus; and as we receive him, including his transforming heart, in Holy Communion. The Heart of Jesus is a fountain of love that fills our hearts and gives us the ability to fulfill our destiny, to love as we have been loved.

As Pope Benedict put it in his letter, underscoring the eucharistic nature of devotion to the Sacred Heart of Jesus,

> The gifts received from the open side, from which "blood and water" flowed (cf. Jn 19:34), ensure that our lives will also become for others a source from which "rivers of living water" flow (Jn 7:38; cf. *DCE* 7). The experience of love, brought by the devotion to the pierced side of the Redeemer, protects us from the risk of withdrawing into ourselves and makes us more ready to live for others. "By this we know love, that he laid down his life for us; and we ought to lay down our lives for the brethren" (1 Jn 3:16; cf. *HA* 38). It was only the experience that God first gave us his love that has enabled us to respond to his commandment of love (cf. *DCE* 17). So it is that the cult of love, which becomes visible in the mystery of the Cross presented anew in every celebration of the Eucharist, lays the foundations of our capacity to love and to make a gift of ourselves (cf. *HA* 69).

Because devotion to the Sacred Heart is grounded in God's love for us and in the Eucharist, the source and summit of the Christian life, it has, in Pope Benedict's words, "an *irreplaceable* importance for our faith and our life of love" and it "remains *indispensable* for a living relationship with God."

Irreplaceable. There is no substitute for this eucharistic devotion. *Indispensable.* It is not passing or optional. It is necessary for a deep and intimate relationship with God. It is necessary in order for us to attain the destiny for which each of us was born.

At the beginning of the third millennium, Blessed John Paul II wrote an apostolic letter *At the Beginning of the New Millennium*

(*Novo Millennio Ineunte*). In it he echoed the call of Jesus to the first apostles, *Duc in altum*, "Put out into the deep" (cf. Lk 5:1–10). It was a call that led to a great catch of fish and the invitation to follow Jesus. Using this as a symbol, Pope John Paul II challenged each of us to go deeper in our spiritual lives, to go deeper in our relationship with Jesus. For the pope, this wasn't a matter of being lukewarm Christians. It was much more serious. As he put it,

> It would be wrong to think that ordinary Christians can be content with a shallow prayer that is unable to fill their whole life. Especially in the face of the many trials to which today's world subjects faith, they would be not only mediocre Christians but "Christians at risk." (*NMI*, 34)

If we don't go deeper in our relationship with God, we won't be able to face the trials that are part and parcel of life. Even more, because the forces of secularization are so strong, we will be at risk of drifting away from the faith.

Building a Civilization of Love

Not only will *we* be at risk, but our *world* will be at risk as well. Humanity has made great advances in technology. There is hope that every disease and illness can be cured and even the aging process itself can be forestalled. Truly humanity has grown in scientific knowledge and the ability to use it for many good things. But often this knowledge has not been used for good but for evil. We have grown in knowledge but not in the wisdom necessary to use that knowledge for what is good. The very things we have created threaten us with a terrible future.

In the last century humanity, drifting away from God, threatened itself with destruction. The possibility of human annihilation remains because the human heart hasn't changed. Sin still hardens human hearts and leads to the destruction of individual lives and the attempted destruction of whole peoples. The twentieth century was the bloodiest century in human history. Technology was used for purposes of mass destruction and genocide. A conversion of heart is required for there to be true change. We need new hearts. We need the Eucharistic and Sacred Heart of Jesus to change our hearts.

Blessed John Paul II wrote of this in a letter that he gave to Fr. Peter-Hans Kolvenbach in 1986 when he made a pilgrimage to Paray-le-Monial.

> In the Heart of Christ the human heart comes to know the true and only meaning of life and destiny, to understand the value of an authentically Christian life, to protect itself from certain perversions, to unite filial love for God with love for the neighbor. In this way—and this is the true meaning of reparation demanded by the Heart of the Savior—on the ruins accumulated through hatred and violence, can be built the civilization of love so greatly desired, the kingdom of the Heart of Christ.

What each individual needs, what the world needs, is love, the love of the Heart of Jesus. As we conclude our reflections, my hope and prayer are that this book will contribute to the awareness of God's devotion to humanity so that we may respond with a devotion that will lead to the transformation of our hearts, our lives, and our world.

Abbreviations

The documents referenced here may be found on the Vatican website: www.vatican.va/phome_en.htm.

AS   *On Consecration to the Sacred Heart (Annum Sacrum).* Encyclical Letter of Pope Leo XIII, 1899.

DCE   *God Is Love (Deus Caritas Est).* Encyclical Letter of Pope Benedict XVI, 2005.

GS   *The Church in the Modern World (Gaudium et Spes).* Vatican Council II, 1965.

HA   *On Devotion to the Sacred Heart (Haurietis Aquas).* Encyclical Letter of Pope Pius XII, 1956.

IDC   *The Unfathomable Riches of Christ (Investigabiles Divitias Christi).* Apostolic Letter of Pope Paul VI, 1965.

LG   *Constitution on the Church (Lumen Gentium).* Vatican Council II, 1964.

MND   *Stay with Us, Lord (Mane Nobiscum Domine).* Apostolic Letter of Pope John Paul II, 2005.

MR   *On Reparation to the Sacred Heart (Miserentissimus Redemptor).* Encyclical Letter of Pope Pius XI, 1928.

NMI   *At the Beginning of the New Millennium (Novo Millennio Ineunte).* Apostolic Letter of Pope John Paul II, 2001.

RVM   *On the Most Holy Rosary (Rosarium Virginis Mariae).* Apostolic Letter of Pope John Paul II, 2002.

SC   *Constitution on the Sacred Liturgy (Sacrosanctum Concilium).* Vatican Council II, 1963.

SCar   *The Sacrament of Charity (Sacramentum Caritatis).* Apostolic Exhortation of Pope Benedict XVI, 2007.

SS   *Saved in Hope (Spe Salvi).* Encyclical Letter of Pope Benedict XVI, 2007.

VD   *Word of the Lord (Verbum Domini).* Apostolic Exhortation of Pope Benedict XVI, 2010.

References

2. The True Love Story

Diadochus, in Office of Readings for Friday in the Second Week in Ordinary Time, *Liturgy of the Hours*.

Joseph Ratzinger, *Behold the Pierced One* (San Francisco: Ignatius Press, 1986), 63.

Ignatius of Loyola, *Spiritual Exercises*, trans. George E. Ganss, S.J. (Chicago: Loyola Press, 1992), 102.

3. The True Love Story Continues

St. Bernard, in Timothy T. O'Donnell, *Heart of the Redeemer* (San Francisco: Ignatius Press, 1992), 94–95.

St. John Chrysostom, in O'Donnell, 88.

St. Justin, in *The Heart of the Saviour: A Symposium on Devotion to the Sacred Heart* by Josef Stierli and Richard Gutzwiller (New York: Herder and Herder, 1957), 45.

St. Irenaeus, in Stierli, 44.

St. Cyprian, in Stierli, 46–47.

St. Gregory the Great, in O'Donnell, 92.

St. Justin, in Stierli, 26.

St. Bonaventure, in O'Donnell, 101.

St. Catherine of Siena, in O'Donnell, 111.

St. Mechthild, in Stierli, 74

St. Francis de Sales, in O'Donnell, 118.

For a more comprehensive history of devotion to the Sacred Heart, see Timothy T. O'Donnell, *Heart of the Redeemer*.

4. Entering into the Heart of the Word

Bruce Marchiano, *In the Footsteps of Jesus* (Eugene, OR: Harvest House Publishers, 1997), 115–116.

Ibid., 77.

5. The Eucharistic Heart of Jesus

Meeting with the Italian Bishops, 2002, "Eucharist, Communion and Solidarity." Accessed at: http://www.vatican.va/roman_curia/congregations/cfaith/documents/rc_con_cfaith_doc_20020602_
ratzinger-eucharistic-congress_en.html.

David L. Fleming. *Discipleship and Its Foundation: A Jesuit Retreat* (St. Louis, MO: Review for Religious Books, 2005).

Thomas Aquinas, *Commentary on the Sentences*.

"Sayings of Abba Joseph of Panephysis, 7," in *Sayings of the Desert Fathers: The Alphabetical Collection*, trans. Benedicta Ward (Kalamazoo, MI: Cistercian Publications, 2006), 103.

6. Reparation

Benedict XVI, *Jesus of Nazareth, Holy Week: From the Entrance into Jerusalem to the Resurrection* (San Francisco: Ignatius Press, 2011), 232.
Ibid., 132–133.
Dietrich Bonhoeffer, *The Cost of Discipleship* (New York: Macmillan, 1979).
Benedict XVI, *Jesus of Nazareth*, 232.
Joseph Ratzinger, *Behold the Pierced One*, 58, 59.

7. Living in Union with the Eucharistic Heart of Jesus

Francis Xavier Nguyen Van Thuan, *Five Loaves and Two Fish* (Washington, DC: Morley Books, 2000), 15.
Walter J. Ciszek, *He Leadeth Me* (New York: Doubleday, 1973), 183.

8. Sacred Heart Devotions

Congregation for Divine Worship and the Discipline of the Sacraments, *Directory on Popular Piety and the Liturgy: Principles and Guidelines* (Vatican City: Libreria Editrice Vaticana, December 2001).
Interview with Admiral Denton. See also Willig's book *Lessons from the School of Suffering: A Young Priest with Cancer Teaches Us How to Live* (Cincinnati, OH: St. Anthony Messenger Press, 2001), 70.
World Youth Day, Madrid, 2011. Accessed at: www.madrid11.com/en/camino/46-catequesis-1-dios-nos-ha-hecho-capaces-de-vivir-con-el.
Letter of Benedict XV, in O'Donnell, 167–168.
John Adams, *The Works of John Adams* (Boston: Little, Brown, 1854), 9:228–229. Accessed at: http://en.wikiquote.org/wiki/John_Adams.

Maria Faustina Kowalska, *Diary: Divine Mercy in My Soul* (Stockbridge, MA: Marian Press, 2003).

Robert A. Stackpole, *Jesus, Mercy Incarnate: St. Faustina and Devotion to Jesus Christ* (Stockbridge, MA: Marian Press, 2003), 108, 110.

James Kubicki, S.J., is the national director of the Apostleship of Prayer, a ministry whose mission is to encourage Christians to make a daily offering of themselves to the Lord and at whose center is the love of the Sacred Heart of Jesus. Kubicki entered the Jesuits in 1971 and was ordained in 1983. Since that time, he has served the Jesuits in numerous capacities including vocations, priestly formation, and deacon and lay ministry formation.

In addition to being a frequent guest on Catholic radio and television, Kubicki is also a popular conference speaker, retreat director, and parish mission speaker. His areas of expertise include the Eucharist, the Sacred Heart of Jesus, the Spiritual Exercises, and the practical spirituality of the Apostleship of Prayer.

Founded in 1865, Ave Maria Press,
a ministry of the Congregation of
Holy Cross, is a Catholic publishing
company that serves the spiritual and
formative needs of the Church and its
schools, institutions, and ministers;
Christian individuals and families; and
others seeking spiritual nourishment.

For a complete listing of titles from

Ave Maria Press

Sorin Books

Forest of Peace

Christian Classics

visit www.avemariapress.com

 ave maria press® / Notre Dame, IN 46556
A Ministry of the United States Province of Holy Cross